NPCA National Park Guide Series

NATIONAL PARKS
AND CONSERVATION AS

GUIDE TO NATIONAL PARKS
ALASKA REGION

Written and compiled by Russell D. Butcher for the National Parks and
Conservation Association and edited by Lynn P. Whitaker

NPCA is America's only private, nonprofit citizen organization dedicated solely
to protecting, preserving, and enhancing the U.S. National Park System. The
association's mission is to protect and enhance America's National Park System
for present and future generations.

Guilford, Connecticut

Photo credits: title page, pages 17, 64–65, 71, 76–77 © David Muench; contents, pages 1, 5, 8–9, 13, 35, 38–39, 41, 53, 56–57, 58, 61, 66–67, 68–69, 74 © Fred Hirschmann; pages 21, 24–25, 43, 50–51, 52, 79, 86 © Carr Clifton; pages 27, 28–29, 31 © Scott T. Smith; page 33 © William Neill/Larry Ulrich Stock; pages 46–47 © Larry Ulrich; page 60 © Jeff Foott

Maps: © Trails Illustrated, a division of National Geographic Maps
Cover and text design: Adam Schwartzman
Cover photo: Denali National Park Alaska (© William Neill/Larry Ulrich Stock)

Library of Congress Cataloging-in-Publication Data

Butcher, Russell D.
    National Parks and Conservation Association guide to national parks: Alaska region / written and compiled by Russell D. Butcher for the National Parks and Conservation Association ; and edited by Lynn P. Whitaker.—1st ed.
        p.   cm. — (NPCA national park guide series)
    ISBN 0-7627-0570-1
    1. Alaska Guidebooks. 2. National parks and preserves—Alaska Guidebooks.
I. Whitaker, Lynn P. II. National Parks and Conservation Association. III. Title. IV. Series.
F902.3.B88 1999
917.804'51—dc21   99–31046
                                                                                  CIP

♻ Printed on recycled paper
Printed and bound in Quebec, Canada
First edition/First printing

National Parks
and Conservation Association

Thomas C. Kiernan
President

Dear Reader:

Welcome to the National Parks and Conservation Association's national park guidebooks—a series designed to help you to discover America's most significant scenery, history, and culture found in the more than 370 areas that make up the U.S. National Park System.

The park system represents the best America has to offer for our natural, historical, and cultural heritage—a collection of resources that we have promised to preserve "unimpaired" for future generations. We hope that, in addition to giving you practical information to help you plan your visits to national park areas, these guides also will help you be a more aware, more responsible visitor to our parks. The cautions offered at the beginning of these guides are not to frighten you away but to remind you that we all have a role in protecting the parks. For it is only if each and every one of us takes responsibility that these special places will be preserved and available for future generations to enjoy.

For more than three-quarters of a century, the National Parks and Conservation Association has been America's leading citizen advocacy group working solely to protect the national parks. Whether fighting to preserve the wilderness character of Cumberland Island National Seashore, preventing the expansion of a major airport outside the Everglades, stopping a coal mine at Cumberland Gap, or defeating legislation that could lead to the closure of many national parks, NPCA has made the voices of its members and supporters heard in efforts to protect the resources of our national parks from harm.

We hope that you will join in our commitment. Remember: when you visit the parks, take only pictures, and leave only footprints.

1776 Massachusetts Avenue, N.W., Washington, D.C. 20036-1904
Telephone (202) 223-NPCA(6722) • Fax (202) 659-0650
♻ PRINTED ON RECYCLED PAPER

CONTENTS

▲ *Fireweed and Mount McKinley in Denali National Park and Preserve, Alaska*

Alaska Region

ABBREVIATIONS

NM	National Monument
NHS	National Historical Park
NM & PRES	National Monument and Preserve
NP	National Park
N PRES	National Preserve
NP & PRES	National Park and Preserve
WR	Wild River

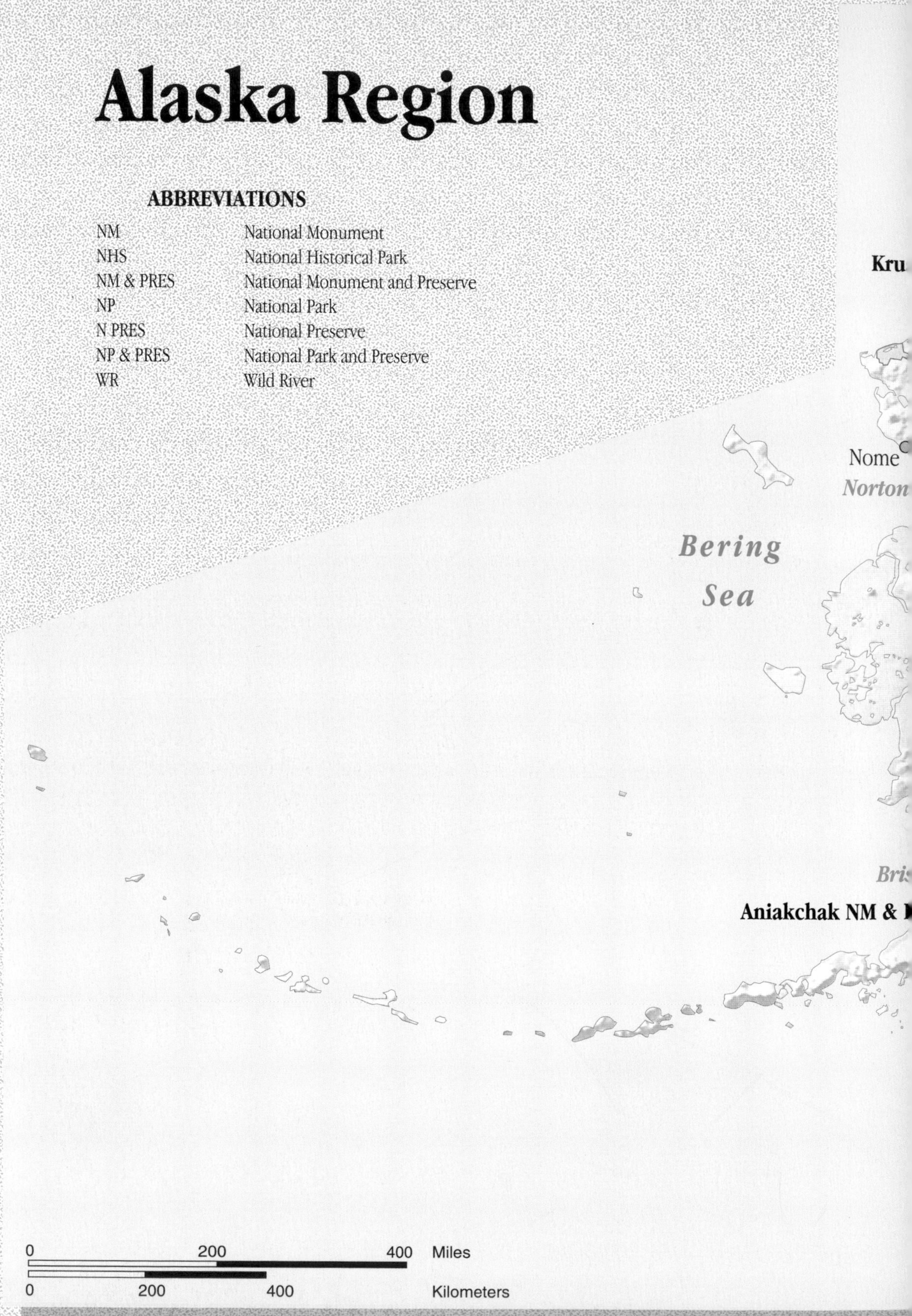

Kru

Nome
Norton

Bering

Sea

Aniakchak NM & I

Bris

0	200	400	Miles

0	200	400	Kilometers

Arctic Ocean

Noatak
N PRES

Kobuk
Valley
NP

Gates of the Arctic
NP & PRES

Land Bridge

Yukon

Yukon–Charley Rivers
N PRES

⑥

Fairbanks

③   ②

Denali NP
& PRES

④

②

①

③

Lake Clark
NP & PRES

①

Anchorage

④

Wrangell–
St. Elias
NP & PRES

Valdez

Klondike
Gold Rush
NHP

①   ⑨

Seward

Homer

Kenai Fjords NP

R

Katmai NP & PRES

Skagway

Gulf of
Alaska

Glacier Bay
NP & PRES

Juneau

Sitka

Sitka NHP

Pacific Ocean

▲ Portage Lake in autumn in Lake Clark National Park and Preserve, Alaska

General Information

Whether you're an American history buff or a bird-watcher, a lover of rocky coastlines or marshy swamps, a dedicated environmentalist or a weekend rambler, and whether you're seeking a way to spend a carefully planned month-long vacation or an unexpectedly free sunny afternoon—the national parks are for you. They offer a broad spectrum of natural and cultural resources in all 50 states as well as Guam, Puerto Rico, the Virgin Islands, and American Samoa where you can learn, exercise, participate in activities, and be constantly moved and inspired by the riches available. Perhaps most important of all, as one of the National Park System's 280 million annual visitors, you become part of the attempt to preserve our natural and historical treasures for present and future generations.

This guidebook will help you do that, as one in a series of eight Regional National Park Guides covering all the units in the National Park System. This section of general information provides both an overview of key facts that can be applied to every unit and a brief history of the National Parks and Conservation Association (NPCA).

SPECIAL PARK PASSES

Some parks charge entrance fees to help offset their operational costs. Several options for special entrance passes are available, enabling you to choose the most appropriate and economical way for you and your family and friends to visit sites.

Park Pass: For this annual entrance permit to a specific fee-charging park, monument, historic site, or recreation area in the National Park System, the cost is usually $10 or $15 depending on the area. Such a pass does not cover any fees other than entrance for permit holder and any accompanying passengers in a private noncommercial vehicle or, in the case of walk-in facilities, the permit holder's spouse, children, and parents. The pass may be purchased in person or by mail from the unit at which it will be used. It is nontransferable and nonrefundable.

Golden Eagle Passport: This annual entrance pass admits visitors to all the federal lands that charge entrance fees; these include national parks, monuments, historic sites, recreation areas, national forests, and national wildlife refuges. The pass costs $50 and is valid for one year from purchase. It does not cover any fees other than entrance for permit holder and any accompanying passengers in a private noncommercial vehicle or, in the case of walk-in facilities, the holder's spouse, children, and parents. The Golden Eagle Passport may be purchased in person or by mail from the National Park Service (NPS), Office of Public Inquiries, Room 1013, U.S. Department of the Interior, 18th & C Streets, N.W., Washington, DC 20240 (202-208-4747) or at any of the seven National Park Service field offices, any of the nine U.S. Forest Service regional offices, or any national park unit and other federal areas that charge an entrance fee. It is nontransferable and nonrefundable.

Golden Age Passport: A one-time $10 fee for this pass allows lifetime entrance to all federal fee-charging areas as described in the Golden Eagle Passport section for citizens and permanent residents of the United States who are 62 years of age or older and any accompanying passengers in a private noncommercial vehicle or, in the case of walk-in facilities, the holder's spouse and children. This pass also entitles the holder to a 50 percent discount on use fees charged in park areas. The Golden Age Passport must be obtained IN PERSON at any of the locations listed in the Golden Eagle Passport section; mail requests are not accepted. Applicants must provide proof of age, such as a driver's license or birth certificate, or sign an affidavit attesting to eligibility.

Golden Access Passport: This free lifetime entrance permit to all federal fee-charging areas as described in the Golden Eagle Passport section is available for citizens and permanent residents of the United States who are visually impaired or permanently disabled and any accompanying passengers in a private noncommercial vehicle or, in the case of walk-in facilities, the permit holder's spouse, children, and parents. It also entitles the holder to a 50 percent discount on use fees charged in park areas. The Golden Access Passport must be obtained IN PERSON at any of the locations listed in the Golden Eagle Passport section; mail requests are not accepted. Applicant must provide proof of eligibility to receive federal benefits or sign an affidavit attesting to one's eligibility.

PASSPORT TO YOUR NATIONAL PARKS

The Passport to Your National Parks is a special commemorative item designed to serve as a companion for park visitors. This informative and unique publication records each visit through special regional and national stamps and cancellations. When you visit any national park, be sure to have your Passport canceled with a rubber stamp marking the name of the park and the date you were there. The Passport gives you the opportunity to share and relive your journey through America's national parks and will become a travel record to cherish for years. Passports cost $4.95; a full set of ten national and regional stamps is $3.95. The national parks represented in the stamp set vary from year to year. For ordering information, call 800-821-2903, or write to Eastern National Park & Monument Association, 110 Hector Street, Suite 105, Conshohocken, PA 19428.

HELPFUL TRIP-PLANNING PUBLICATIONS

Two volumes offer descriptive text on the National Park System: Exploring Our National Parks and Monuments, by Devereux Butcher (ninth edition by Russell D. Butcher), and Exploring Our National Historic Parks and Sites, by Russell D. Butcher. These books feature descriptions and black-and-white photographs of more than 370 National Park System units. Both volumes also contain chapters on possible new parks, threats to the parks, a history of NPCA, and the national park standards. To

order, contact Roberts Rinehart Publishers, 6309 Monarch Park Place, Niwot, CO 80503; 800-352-1985 or 303-530-4400.

NPCA offers the following brochures at no charge: "The National Parks: How to Have a Quality Experience" and "Visiting Battlefields: The Civil War". These brochures provide helpful information on how best to enjoy a visit to the national parks. NPCA members can also receive the Park System Map and Guide, The National Parks Index, The National Parks Camping Guide, and Lesser Known Areas as part of NPCA's PARK-PAK by calling 202-223-6722, ext. 214.

The Story Behind the Scenery® and *The Continuing Story*® series are lavishly illustrated books providing informative text and magnificent photographs of the landscapes, flora, and fauna of our national parklands. More than 100 titles on the national parks, historic events, and Indian cultures, as well as an annual national parks calendar, are available. For information, call toll free 800-626-9673, fax to 702-731-9421, or write to KC Publications, 3245 E. Patrick Lane, Suite A, Las Vegas, NV 89120.

The National Parks: Index and *Lesser Known Areas*, both produced by the National Park Service, can be ordered by contacting the Superintendent of Documents, U.S. Government Printing Office, Washington, DC 20402-9325; 202-512-1800. To receive at no charge the *National Park System Map and Guide*, the *National Trails System Map and Guide*; or an *Official Map and Guide* of specific national parks, contact National Park Service, Office of Information, P.O. Box 37127, Washington, DC 20013-7127; 202-208-4747.

National Parks Visitor Facilities and Services is a directory of vendors authorized to serve park visitors through contracts with the National Park Service. Concessionaires offering lodging, food, beverages, outfitting, tours, trail rides, and other activities and services are listed alphabetically. To order, contact the National Park Hospitality Association, 1331 Pennsylvania Avenue, N.W., Suite 724, Washington, DC 20004; 202-662-7097.

Great Walks, Inc., publishes six pocket-sized books of detailed information on specific trails in Yosemite; Sequoia and Kings Canyon in California; Big Bend; Great Smoky Mountains; and Acadia and Mount Desert Island in Maine. For information, send $1 (refundable with your first order) to Great Walks, P.O. Box 410, Goffstown, NH 03045.

The U.S. Bureau of Land Management (BLM) offers free maps that detail recreation areas and scenic and backcountry roads and trails. These are available by contacting the BLM at the Department of the Interior, 1849 C Street,

N.W., Suite 5600, Washington, DC 20240; 202-452-5125. In addition, *Beyond the National Parks: A Recreational Guide to Public Lands in the West,* published by the Smithsonian Institution Press, is an informative guidebook to many special places administered by BLM. *America's Secret Recreation Areas,* by Michael Hodgson, is an excellent resource for little-known natural areas in 12 Western states. It details 270 million acres of land administered by BLM, with campgrounds, recreational activities, trails, maps, facilities, and much more. The 1995-96 edition is published by Foghorn Press and is

▲ *Bering Land Bridge National Preserve, Alaska*

available for $17.95 by calling 1-800-FOGHORN.

The National Wildlife Refuge Visitors Guide can be ordered free from the U.S. Fish and Wildlife Service's Publications Unit at 4401 North Fairfax Drive, MS 130 Webb, Arlington, VA 22203; 703-358-1711.

The four-volume *Birds of the National Parks,* by Roland H. Wauer, a retired NPS interpreter and biologist, provides an excellent reference on the parks' birds and their seasons and habitats. This series, written for the average rather than specialist park visitor, is unfortunately out of print.

SAFETY AND REGULATIONS

To protect the national parks' natural and cultural resources and the millions of people who come to enjoy them, the National Park Service asks every visitor to abide by some important regulations. Park staffs do all they can to help you have a safe and pleasant visit, but your cooperation is essential.

Some park hazards—deep lakes, sheer cliffs, extremely hot or cold temperatures—cannot be eliminated. However, accidents and illnesses can be prevented if you use the same common sense you would at home and become familiar with the park. Take some time before your trip or when you first arrive to get to know the park's regulations, warnings, and potential hazards. If you have children, make sure they understand such precautions, and keep a careful watch over them, especially in potentially dangerous situations. If you are injured or become ill, the staff can help by directing you to the nearest medical center and, in some parks, by giving you emergency care.

A few rules and safety tips are common to many parks. At all parks, you must keep your campsite clean and the park free of litter by disposing of refuse in trash receptacles. The National Park Service also asks you to follow federal regulations and refrain from the abuse of alcohol and the use of drugs, which are often contributing factors to injuries and deaths. Other rules and safety tips are outlined in the "Special Advisories and Visitor Ethics" section; more detailed information may be provided in park brochures, on signs, and on bulletin boards at camping areas and other park sites. The National Park Service asks that you report any violation of park regulations to park authorities. If you have any questions, seek the advice of a ranger.

SAFETY AND REGULATIONS

Safe Driving

Park roads are designed for sight-seeing, not speeding. Because roads are often narrow and winding and sometimes steep, visitors should drive carefully, observe posted speed limits, and be alert for wildlife, pedestrians, bicyclists, other drivers, fallen rocks or trees, slippery roads, and other hazards. Be especially alert for motorists who might stop unexpectedly for sight-seeing or wildlife viewing. Visitors are urged to use roadside pullouts instead of stopping on the roadway.

Campfires

Most parks permit fires, as long as certain rules are followed. To avoid a wildfire that would be dangerous to people, property, and natural resources, parks may allow only certain types of campfires—fires only in grills provided, for example, or in designated fire rings. Firewood gathering may be prohibited or restricted to certain areas, so visitors should plan on bringing their own fuel supply. Fires should be kept under control, should never be left unattended, and should be thoroughly extinguished before departure.

Quiet Hours

Out of respect for other visitors, campers should keep noise to a minimum at all times, especially from 10 p.m. to 6 a.m.

Pets

Pets must always be leashed or otherwise physically restrained for the protection of the animal, other visitors, and wildlife. Pets may be prohibited from certain areas, including public buildings, trails, and the backcountry. A few parks prohibit pets altogether. Dog owners are responsible for keeping their pets quiet in camping areas and elsewhere. Guide dogs are exempted from park restrictions. Some parks provide kennel services; contact the park visitor center for information.

Protection of Valuables

Theft is just as much a problem in the national parks as elsewhere, so when leaving a campsite or heading out on a trail, visitors should take valuables along or hide them out of sight in a locked vehicle, preferably in the trunk.

Heat, Cold, and Other Hazards

Visitors should take precautions to deal with the demands and hazards of a park environment. On hot days, pace yourself, schedule strenuous activities for the morning and evening hours, and drink plenty of water and other fluids. On cold days or if you get cold and wet, frostbite and the life-threatening illness called hypothermia can occur, so avoid subjecting yourself to these conditions for long periods. In the thinner air of mountains and high plateaus, even those tasks easy to perform at home can leave one short of breath and dizzy; the best advice is to slow down. If a thunderstorm occurs, avoid exposed areas and open bodies of water, where lightning often strikes, and keep out of low-lying areas and stream beds, where flash floods are most likely to occur.

Wild Plants and Animals

It is the responsibility of every visitor to help preserve the native plants and animals protected in the parks: leave them as you find them, undisturbed and safe. Hunting or carrying a loaded weapon is prohibited in all national parks and national monuments. Hunting during the designated season is allowed in parts of only a few National Park System areas, such as national recreation areas, national preserves, and national seashores and lakeshores. While biting insects or toxic plants, such as poison ivy or poison oak, are the most likely danger you will encounter, visitors should be aware of hazards posed by other wild plants and animals. Rattlesnakes, ticks, and animals carrying rabies or other transmittable diseases, for instance, inhabit some parks. Any wild creature—whether it is as large as a bison or moose or as small as a raccoon or prairie dog—is unpredictable and should be viewed from a distance. Remember that feeding any wild animal is absolutely prohibited.

Campers should especially guard against attracting bears to their campsites as a close encounter with a grizzly, brown, or black bear can result in serious injury or death. Park officials in bear country recommend, and often require, that campers take certain precautions. One is to keep a campsite clean. Bears' sensitive noses can easily detect food left on cans, bottles, and utensils or even personal items with food-like odors (toothpaste, deodorant, etc.). Second, food items should be stored in containers provided by the parks or in your vehicle, preferably out of sight in the trunk. Bears, especially those in Yosemite, are adept at breaking into cars and other motor vehicles containing even small amounts of food and can cause extensive damage to motor vehicles

as they attempt to reach what they can smell. Third, in the backcountry, food should be hung from poles or wires that are provided or from a tree; visitors should inquire at the park as to the recommended placement. In treeless surroundings, campers should store food at least 50 yards from any campsite. If bears inhabit a park on your itinerary, ask the National Park Service for a bear brochure with helpful tips on avoiding trouble in bear country and inquire if bears are a problem where you plan to hike or camp.

Backcountry Camping

Camping in the remote backcountry of a park requires much more preparation than other camping. Most parks require that you pick up a backcountry permit before your trip so that rangers will know about your plans. They can also advise you of hazards and regulations and give you up-to-date information on road, trail, river, lake, or sea conditions, weather forecasts, special fire regulations, availability of water, and other matters. Backcountry permits are available at visitor centers, headquarters, and ranger stations.

There are some basic rules to follow whenever you camp in the backcountry: stay on the trails; pack out all trash; obey fire regulations; be prepared for sudden and drastic weather changes; carry a topographic map or nautical chart when necessary; and carry plenty of food and water. In parks where water is either unavailable or scarce, you may need to carry as much as one gallon of water per person per day. In other parks, springs, streams, or lakes may be abundant, but always purify water before drinking it. Untreated water can carry contaminants. One of the most common, especially in Western parks, is *giardia*, an organism that causes an unpleasant intestinal illness. Water may have to be boiled or purified with tablets; check with the park staff for the most effective treatment.

Sanitation

Visitors should bury human waste six to eight inches below ground and a minimum of 100 feet from a watercourse. Waste water should be disposed of at least 100 feet from a watercourse or campsite. Do not wash yourself, your clothing, or your dishes in any watercourse.

CAMPING RESERVATIONS

Most campsites are available on a first-come, first-served basis, but many sites can be reserved through the National Park Reservation Service. For reservations at Acadia, Assateague Island, Cape Hatteras, Channel Islands, Chickasaw, Death Valley, Everglades, Glacier, Grand Canyon, Great Smoky Mountains, Greenbelt, Gulf Islands, Joshua Tree, Katmai, Mount Rainier, Rocky Mountain, Sequoia-Kings Canyon, Sleeping Bear Dunes, Shenandoah, Whiskeytown, and Zion, call 800-365-CAMP. For reservations for Yosemite National Park, call 800-436-PARK. Reservations can also be made at any of these parks in person. Currently, reservations can be made as much as eight weeks in advance or up to the day before the start of a camping stay. Please have credit card and detailed camping information available when you call in order to facilitate the reservation process.

BIOSPHERE RESERVES AND WORLD HERITAGE SITES

A number of the national park units have received international recognition by the United Nations Educational, Scientific and Cultural Organization for their superlative natural and/or cultural values. Biosphere Reserves are representative examples of diverse natural landscapes, with both a fully protected natural core or park unit and surrounding land being managed to meet human needs. World Heritage Sites include natural and cultural sites with "universal" values that illustrate significant geological processes, may be crucial to the survival of threatened plants and animals, or demonstrate outstanding human achievement.

A Brief History

▲ *Creek cascading toward the Taiya River in Klondike Gold Rush National Historical Park, Alaska*

A Brief History of the National Parks and Conservation Association

In 1916, when Congress established the National Park Service to administer the then nearly 40 national parks and monuments, the agency's first director, Stephen Tyng Mather, quickly saw the need for a private organization, independent of the federal government, to be the citizens' advocate for the parks.

Consequently, on May 19, 1919, the National Parks Association—later renamed the National Parks and Conservation Association (NPCA)—was founded in Washington, D.C. The National Park Service's former public relations director, Robert Sterling Yard, was named to lead the new organization—a position he held for a quarter century.

The association's chief objectives were then and continue to be the following: to vigorously oppose threats to the integrity of the parks; to advocate worthy and consistent standards of *national* significance for the addition of new units to the National Park System; and, through a variety of educational means, to promote the public understanding and appreciation of the parks. From the beginning, threats to the parks have been a major focus of the organization. One of the biggest conservation battles of NPCA's earliest years erupted in 1920, when Montana irrigation interests advocated building a dam and raising the level of Yellowstone Lake in Yellowstone National Park. Fortunately, this threat to the world's first national park was ultimately defeated—the first landmark victory of the fledgling citizens' advocacy group on behalf of the national parks.

At about the same time, a controversy developed over the authority given to the Water Power Commission (later renamed the Federal Power Commission) to authorize the construction of hydropower projects in national parks. The commission had already approved the flooding of Hetch Hetchy Valley in Yosemite National Park. In the ensuing political struggle, NPCA pushed for an amendment to the water power law that would prohibit such projects in all national parks. A compromise produced only a partial victory: the ban applied to the parks then in existence, but not to parks yet to be established. As a result, each new park's enabling legislation would have to expressly stipulate that the park was exempt from the commission's authority to develop hydropower projects. Yet this success, even if partial, was significant.

Also in the 1920s, NPCA successfully urged establishment of new national parks: Shenandoah, Great Smoky Mountains, Carlsbad Caverns, Bryce Canyon, and a park that later became Kings Canyon, as well as an expanded Sequoia. The association also pushed to expand Yellowstone, Grand Canyon, and Rocky Mountain national parks, pointing out that "the boundaries of the older parks were often established arbitrarily, following ruler lines drawn in far-away offices." The association continues to advocate such topographically and ecologically oriented boundary improvements for many parks.

In 1930, the establishment of Colonial National Historical Park and the George Washington Birthplace National Monument signaled a broadening of the National Park System to places of primarily historical rather than environmental importance. A number of other historical areas, such as Civil War battlefields, were soon transferred from U.S. military jurisdiction to the National Park Service, and NPCA accurately predicted that this new category of parks "will rapidly surpass, in the number of units, its world-celebrated scenic" parks. Today, there are roughly 200 historical parks out of the total of 378 units. NPCA also pushed to add other units, including Everglades National Park, which was finally established in 1947.

A new category of National Park System units was initiated with the establishment of Cape Hatteras National Seashore in North Carolina. However, in spite of NPCA opposition, Congress permitted public hunting in the seashore—a precedent that subsequently opened the way to allow this consumptive resource use in other national seashores, national lakeshores, national rivers, and national preserves. With the exception of traditional, subsistence hunting in Alaska national preserves, NPCA continues to oppose hunting in all national parks and monuments.

In contrast to its loss at Cape Hatteras, NPCA achieved a victory regarding Kings Canyon National Park as a result of patience and tenacity. When the park was established in 1940, two valleys—Tehipite and Cedar Grove—were left out of the park as a concession to hydroelectric power and irrigation interests. A few years later, however, as the result of concerted efforts by the association and other environmental groups, these magnificently scenic valleys were added to the park.

In 1942, the association took a major step in its public education mission when it began publishing *National Parks*. This award-winning, full-color magazine contains news, editorials, and feature articles that help to inform members about the parks, threats facing them, and opportunities for worthy new parks and offers readers a chance to participate in the protection and enhancement of the National Park System.

In one of the most heavily publicized park-protection battles of the 1950s, NPCA and other groups succeeded in blocking construction of two hydroelectric power dams that would have inundated the spectacularly scenic river canyons in Dinosaur National Monument. In the 1960s, an even bigger battle erupted over U.S. Bureau of Reclamation plans to build two dams in the Grand Canyon. But with the cooperative efforts of a number of leading environmental organizations and tremendous help from the news media, these schemes were defeated, and Grand Canyon National Park was expanded.

In 1980, the National Park System nearly tripled in size with the passage of the Alaska National Interest Lands Conservation Act (ANILCA). One of the great milestones in the history of American land conservation, ANILCA established ten new, and expanded three existing, national park units in Alaska. This carefully crafted compromise also recognized the special circumstances of Alaska and authorized subsistence hunting, fishing, and gathering by rural residents as well as special access provisions on most units. The challenge of ANILCA is to achieve a balance of interests that are often in conflict. Currently, NPCA is working to protect sensitive park areas and wildlife from inappropriate development of roads and unregulated motorized use, and to ensure that our magnificent national parks in Alaska always offer the sense of wildness, discovery, and adventure that Congress intended.

In 1981, the association sponsored a conference to address serious issues affecting the welfare of the National Park System. The following year, NPCA published a book on this theme called *National Parks in Crisis*. In the 1980s and 1990s, as well, the association sponsored its nationwide "March for Parks" program in conjunction with Earth Day in April. Money raised from the hundreds of marches funds local park projects, including improvement and protection priorities and educational projects in national, state, and local parks.

NPCA's landmark nine-volume document, *National Park System Plan,* was issued in 1988. It contained proposals for new parks and park expansions, assessments of threats to park resources and of research needs, explorations of the importance of interpretation to the visitor's quality of experience, and issues relating to the internal organization of the National Park Service. Two years later, the two-volume *Visitor Impact Management* was released. This document found favor within the National Park Service because of its pragmatic discussions of "carrying capacity" and visitor-impact management methodology and its case studies. In 1993, *Park Waters in Peril* was released, focusing on threats seriously jeopardizing water resources and presenting a dozen case studies.

The association has become increasingly concerned about the effect of noise on the natural quiet in the parks. NPCA has helped formulate restrictions on flightseeing tours over key parts of the Grand Canyon; urged special restrictions on tour flights over Alaska's national parks; supported a ban on tour flights over other national parks such as Yosemite; expressed opposition to plans for construction of major new commercial airports close to Mojave National Preserve and Petroglyph National Monument; opposed the recreational use of snowmobiles in some parks and advocated restrictions on their use in others; and supported regulations prohibiting the use of personal watercraft on lakes in national parks.

Other association activities of the late 20th century have included helping to block development of a major gold mining operation that could have seriously impaired Yellowstone National Park; opposing a coal mine near

Zion National Park that would have polluted Zion Canyon's North Fork of the Virgin River; objecting to proposed lead mining that could pollute the Ozark National Scenic Riverways; opposing a major waste dump adjacent to Joshua Tree National Park; and helping to defeat a proposed U.S. Department of Energy nuclear waste dump adjacent to Canyonlands National Park and on lands worthy of addition to the park. NPCA is currently proposing the completion of this national park with the addition of 500,000 acres. This proposal to double the size of the park would extend protection across the entire Canyonlands Basin. NPCA has also continued to work with the Everglades Coalition and others to help formulate meaningful ways of restoring the seriously impaired Everglades ecosystem; is urging protection of New Mexico's geologically and scenically outstanding Valles Caldera, adjacent to Bandelier National Monument; and is pushing for the installation of scrubbers on air-polluting coal-fired power plants in the Midwest and upwind from the Grand Canyon.

The association, in addition, is continuing to seek meaningful solutions to traffic congestion and urbanization on the South Rim of the Grand Canyon and in Yosemite Valley; is opposing construction of a six-lane highway through Petroglyph National Monument that would destroy sacred Native American cultural assets; and is fighting a plan to build a new road through Denali National Park. NPCA has supported re-establishment of such native wildlife as the gray wolf at Yellowstone and desert bighorn sheep at Capitol Reef and other desert parks, as well as urging increased scientific research that will enable the National Park Service to more effectively protect natural ecological processes in the future. The association is also continuing to explore a proposal to combine Organ Pipe Cactus National Monument and Cabreza Prieta National Wildlife Refuge into a Sonoran Desert National Park, possibly in conjunction with Mexico's Pinacate Biosphere Reserve.

In 1994, on the occasion of NPCA's 75th anniversary, the association sponsored a major conference on the theme "Citizens Protecting America's Parks: Joining Forces for the Future." As a result, NPCA became more active in recruiting a more racially and socially diverse group of park protectors. Rallying new constituencies for the parks helped NPCA in 1995 to defeat a bill that would have called for Congress to review national parks for possible closure. NPCA was also instrumental in the passage of legislation to establish the National Underground Railroad Network to Freedom.

In January 1999, NPCA hosted another major conference, this time focusing on the need for the park system, and the Park Service itself, to be relevant, accessible, and open to all Americans. The conference led to the creation of a number of partnership teams between national parks and minority communities. In conjunction with all this program activity, the association experienced its greatest growth in membership, jumping from about 24,000 in 1980 to nearly 400,000 in the late 1990s.

As NPCA and its committed Board of Trustees, staff, and volunteers face the challenges of park protection in the 21st century, the words of the association's past president, Wallace W. Atwood, in 1929 are as timely now as then:

> All who join our association have the satisfaction that comes only from unselfish acts; they will help carry forward a consistent and progressive program . . . for the preservation and most appropriate utilization of the unique wonderlands of our country. Join and make this work more effective.

Each of us can help nurture one of the noblest endeavors in the entire history of mankind—the national parks idea that began so many years ago at Yellowstone and has spread and blossomed around the world. Everyone can help make a difference in determining just how well we succeed in protecting the priceless and irreplaceable natural and cultural heritage of the National Park System and passing it along unimpaired for the generations to come.

INTRODUCTION TO ALASKA AND ITS PARKS

▲ *Mount St. Elias in Wrangell–St. Elias National Park and Preserve, Alaska*

Introduction to Alaska and Its Parks

Alaska is blessed with some of the world's most exceptional national parks, encompassing environments from broad tundra plains to mountain ranges of staggering proportions, from coastline marked with fjords and glaciers to lush rainforests and sand dunes. Because of the remote nature of many of Alaska's parks, the means of getting to the parks and the facilities available are quite different from national parks in what Alaskans call the "lower 48." To help make your visit to Alaska's parklands the most rewarding experience possible, therefore, it is important to familiarize yourself with a number of special regulations and precautions to ensure both your own safety and the preservation of this unique environment.

FLORA AND FAUNA

Because many of the arctic and subarctic plants in Alaska are fragile and take many years to grow, do leave them undisturbed so others may enjoy them. Berry picking and mushroom hunting are Alaskan traditions, but be sure you know what you have found before eating these wild foods.

Any wild creature is unpredictable, whether it is as large as a moose or as small as a ground squirrel. It is important for visitors to try to have as little impact as possible on these creatures and their environment. Under no circumstance is the feeding of animals allowed, and garbage or food should never be left accessible to animals. Such action is subject to fines and even jail time. The main reason for these precautions is that, if an animal becomes accustomed to being fed, it almost always becomes a problem and eventually must be destroyed.

Virtually every park in Alaska has bears. Close encounters with Alaskan brown grizzly bears and black bears can all be potentially dangerous situations—not only for the person, but for the bear as well. Precautions must therefore be taken when traveling or camping in bear country. When hiking, avoid dense brush that obscures your view, as hiking in such areas creates the potential for a surprise encounter in which bears tend to react defensively. Should you have to travel in such areas, make lots of noise by singing, clapping, or talking loudly. Shrill noises should be avoided. Under no circumstance should you approach a bear. If you encounter a bear, try to back away slowly and avoid sudden movements. If the bear charges, stand your ground. If needed, assume the fetal position with your hands clasped over the back of your neck, and use your backpack as a barrier between you and the bear. The use of mace or pepper spray is not a sure means of warding off bear attacks especially if used improperly, so be sure to read thoroughly the directions for use. Because results from such products are mixed, they should be used only when no other options are available.

A clean campsite with food properly stored in bear-resistant food containers (BRFC) is the best means of avoiding an encounter. These containers are essential in Alaska's backcountry. When setting up camp, make sure that your cooking site, tent, and BRFC are at least all 100 yards apart. Also, avoid bringing food or other aromatic items such as toothpaste and deodorant into the tent; store these items with your food.

In addition to bears, moose can be dangerous animals. In the fall, during the rut, bull moose are also potentially dangerous animals. Bulls injured during the rut are especially dangerous because of their unpredictability. The most important moose to avoid, however, is probably a cow moose with young; their protective instincts and great strength are excellent reasons to always be aware of your surroundings. When hiking in dense willows, be sure to look out for moose and do your best to avoid them. If you encounter one, move away quickly to avoid being trampled under foot. Moose generally inflict injury with powerful kicks or, in the case of bull moose, with their antlers.

RIVER CROSSINGS

Many areas in Alaska have glacially fed rivers with a milky appearance, complicating river crossings because it is difficult to gauge their depth. The water is often fast flowing and always cold, and the water level can change dramatically during the course of a day as more melting occurs. Although this phenomenon occurs especially on warm days, on cooler rainy days the levels can also be dramatically affected. In addition, the nature of a braided stream is such that it constantly changes course, making it difficult to establish a crossing point.

Although experience is your best guide to river crossings, the following are some hints to make your crossing as safe as possible. First, if you don't feel comfortable with your ability to read the river or if the river is just too big, don't cross it. Second, bring an old pair of shoes with which to cross rivers. Proper footwear is essential because large rocks can be tumbling down the river unseen and shoes provide extra traction and stability. A stout walking stick is another good tool; not only does it help with balance, but it is useful in gauging the depth of the river. Third, pack essentials in waterproof bags. If there are several crossings on your route, consider taking such measures for all of your water-sensitive gear. If you are solo hiking, this precaution is essential. Fourth, spend some time on your approach to the river looking for potential routes. Look for areas where the river is wider and slower, and beware of areas where the bank has recently eroded, as often the water can be flowing faster and deeper in these sections. Fifth, as you prepare to cross the river, unbuckle the waist and chest straps on your backpack, and leave the shoulder straps loose. Should you fall while crossing the river, the ability to shed your pack will keep you from getting dragged down. Cross the river moving slightly up stream because moving with the water can make for unstable footing. If crossing as a group, link arms and cross in a line parallel to the flow of the water. Should you or a member of your party get wet during the crossing, be aware of the potential for hypothermia. Finally, when camping on river bars, take the weather into consideration as you set up camp. Camp away from recently eroded river banks, as channels can change quickly and without warning.

Travelers to Alaska must be sure to educate themselves about the warning signs and methods of treating hypothermia, as Alaska's sub-arctic and arctic climates create the potential for snowfall at any time of year as well as unpredictable and sudden changes in the weather. The need to be prepared for the unexpected doesn't mean you need to carry a parka with you in the summer, but if you travel in Alaska's backcountry, you need to be knowledgeable. Hypothermia can be a problem at almost any temperature, especially if it is compounded by dehydration or lack of nourishment.

Early stages of hypothermia exhibit marked changes in mental status (irritability, poor decision making, slurred speech), uncontrollable shivering, or exhaustion. If you or someone in your party starts to get cold, take the time to warm up. If an individual gets wet by immersion or perspiration, be sure to get the person into dry clothes as soon as possible. High energy foods, warm sweet liquids, and strenuous exercise can ward off the beginnings of mild hypothermia. As hypothermia advances, the signs become more exaggerated, and the body cannot produce enough heat by itself. Heat from external sources is needed to warm the shell of the body, so blood returning to the core from the extremities doesn't further cool the core. If a hypothermic person stops shivering and the person's mental status has further declined, the advanced stages of hypothermia have begun. Under no circumstances should alcohol be consumed by the hypothermic person as it acts as a sedative and will slow the heart rate, which reduces blood flow to critical areas of the body and advances the hypothermic condition. In the final stage of hypothermia, there is a rush of blood from the core of the body to the extremities, and the person will suddenly seem to recover, usually shedding clothes and regaining some of the lost mental status; however, the person may then die shortly thereafter. The earlier a problem is recognized, the easier it is to prevent the advancement of hypothermia into the more severe life-threatening stages.

OTHER PRECAUTIONS

Hunting or carrying a loaded weapon is prohibited in most parks. State permits are required and regulations must be followed.

Most parks also require that you obtain a backcountry camping permit in preparation for your trip. This process allows rangers to know about your plans so that they can advise you of hazards and regulations as well as give you up-to-date information on the area. These permits can be acquired at visitor centers and ranger stations.

CHECKLIST FOR HIKING AND CAMPING

Equipment:

Daypack or back pack
Water bottles
Sleeping bag with pad or air mattress
Cooking pots, eating utensils, can opener (if needed)
Tent (preferably free standing)
Biodegradable soap
Tarp or ground cloth
Small towel (can double as a potholder)
Lightweight stove and extra fuel
Toothbrush
Insect repellant and set or headnet
Electrolyte replacement for plain water (Tang,Gatorade, etc.)
First-aid kit (know how to use it)
Plastic trash bags (large bags can double as a pack cover in wet weather)
Pocket knife
Flashlight or headlamp with spare batteries and bulb
Waterproof matches and/or lighter
Toilet paper (remember to pack out all paper trash)
Digging tool for toilet needs
Sunglasses, lip balm, and sunscreen (especially important if traveling on snow)
Topographic map and compass (magnetic declination varies from 27° to 37° east in Alaska)
Pump-type water filter or purification tablets

Optional/Recommended:

Walking stick (telescoping type recommended)
Sewing kit
Binoculars
Signal mirror
Candle or lantern (not needed for most summer months)
Nylon cord (50 feet)

Clothing:

Hiking boots
Fleece or pile jacket or wool sweater
Light footwear (shoes for river crossing recommended)
Hat or cap
Reliable rain gear (jacket and pants)
Light wool or polypro gloves/mittens
Windbreaker (optional, raincoat can double as this)
Long-sleeve shirt (no cotton)
Polypropelene thermal underwear (light to medium weight)
T-shirt
Wool or other insulating synthetic socks (no cotton)
Underwear
Long pants and/or shorts (long underwear with shorts can double as long pants)

A few essentials:

Well-insulated boots (shoepacks, bunny boots)
Doubled pairs of socks
Insulated hat
Heavyweight thermal underwear
Insulated snow pants
Parka with hood (down is warm but synthetic fibers retain their loft)
Mittens with waterproof covers

* Appropriate winter clothing varies greatly with temperature and activity. Multiple layers of clothing are necessary for outdoor activities such as cross-country skiing. When active, be aware of overheating, as perspiration can dampen clothing and reduce insulative properties. Bulkier clothing with more insulation is appropriate for dog mushing or situations where aerobic activity is limited.

Denali National Park and Preserve

▲ Mount McKinley and cottonwood trees

Denali National Park and Preserve

P.O. Box 9
Denali Park, AK 99755-0009
907-683-2294

Taking its name from the Athabascan Indian name for Mount McKinley, "the High One," this 4,741,800-acre national park and adjacent 1,334,200-acre national preserve in Southcentral Alaska protects a vast wilderness of ice- and snow-covered peaks, open tundra, spruce-forested areas known as taiga, and valleys with braided, glacier-fed rivers. Stretching for more than 100 miles along the southern part of the park is the massive Alaska Range, dominated by majestic Mount McKinley—its 20,320-foot-high summit the highest point in North America. Broad expanses of the park are covered with low-growing willows and dwarf birches, and pure stands of spruce trees grow in river valleys. Wooded areas elsewhere consist of spruce, aspen, paper birch, and balsam poplar. Carpets of wildflowers bloom from June to mid-July, while late August and early September are aglow with the yellow of birch, willow, and aspen and the red of blueberry and bearberry bushes and fireweed. There are a variety of autumn berries, such as blueberries, cranberries, and crowberries. The diversity of habitats supports an abundance of wildlife—notably grizzly bears, caribou, moose, Dall sheep, gray wolf, and more than 150 species of birds.

The national park was established in 1917; it was designated a Biosphere Reserve in 1976; and the park was tripled in size in 1980.

OUTSTANDING FEATURES

Among the many outstanding features of the park are the following: **Mount McKinley,** the park's awesome centerpiece which, in spite of such life-threatening risks as frostbite, dehydration, hypothermia, and avalanche, annually challenges more than a thousand climbers from all over the world; **Sable Pass,** an area on the park road where visitors can often see grizzly bears feeding on berries and roots; **Polychrome Pass,** another area on the park road which affords a magnificent view southward of the Alaska Range, weather permitting; **Stony Hill Overlook,** a spot on the park road where visitors can sometimes see caribou as well as get a great view of Mount McKinley, weather permitting; **Muldrow Glacier,** a river of ice that extends 35 miles through a gorge and across the tundra to within a mile of the park road; **Sheldon Amphitheatre,** the area where legendary bush pilot Don Sheldon made countless glacier landings; and **Wonder Lake,** a body of water famous for its views of wading moose and of Mount McKinley, weather permitting.

PRACTICAL INFORMATION

When to Go

The park road is open from early June to mid-September. Year-round use is limited to independent backcountry skiing. Visitor facilities are limited during the winter as most visitors come between late May and mid-September, when days are longer (more than 20 hours of daylight in June) and temperatures are milder. The tundra comes to life in early June (along with a healthy mosquito population), so if the flora of the subarctic is of interest to you, this is the best time to come. The avian population also begins to flourish at that time. June, in general, is usually less crowded than July and August and is a wonderful time to visit. July is generally warm with a wide variety of weather and attracts the most visitors. August and September offer the rich fall colors of the tundra. The fall, which generally has good weather although it can snow at any time, is probably the best time to view wildlife because of the increased activity before winter. Park concessioners offer day and overnight dogsled trips during the winter.

How to Get There

By Car: From Anchorage, take the George Parks Highway north 240 miles. From Fairbanks, take the George Parks Highway south 120 miles.

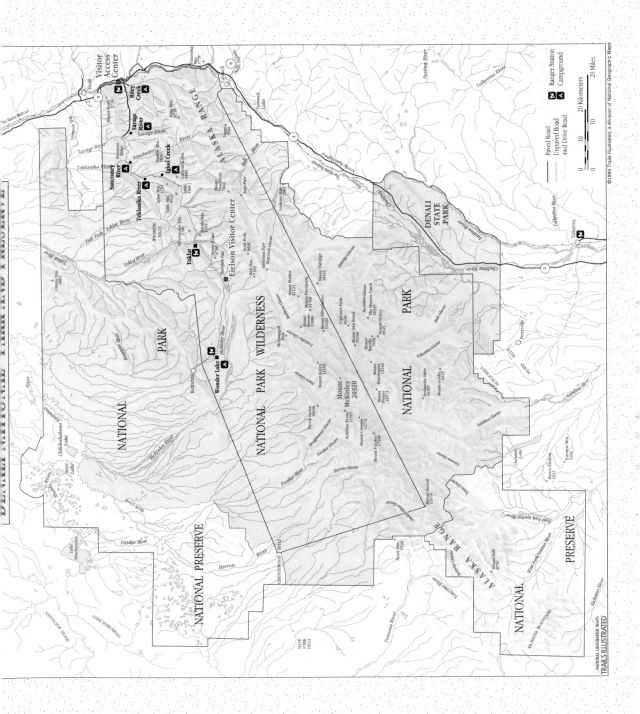

NATIONAL GEOGRAPHIC MAPS
TRAILS ILLUSTRATED

▲ *Tundra Pond and Mount McKinley in Denali National Park and Preserve, Alaska*

By Air: Anchorage and Fairbanks International Airports (907-266-2437 and 907-474-2500) are served by most major airlines. There are also airstrips in Healy and Cantwell, which are served only by charter flights in small aircraft from Anchorage and Fairbanks.

By Train: The Alaska Railroad (800-544-0552) offers service between Anchorage and Fairbanks by way of Denali National Park. The train station is inside the park, about a mile from the park entrance. Many park visitors arrive by rail.

By Bus: Gray Line of Alaska (800-544-2206) serves Denali from Anchorage and Fairbanks in the summer. Other bus lines include Moon Bay Express (907-274-6454), Alaska Direct (800-780-6652), and Denali Express (800-327-7651).

Fees and Permits

Entrance fees are $5 per person or $10 per family, valid for seven consecutive days. Free backcountry permits for overnight camping must be obtained in person at the visitor access center in summer and at park headquarters in winter. A state license is required in the park additions and the preserve for sport fishing. No state license is required in the Denali Wilderness although fishing is limited. Hunting is permitted in the preserve with a state license. Permits are required for commercial activities conducted in the park or preserve.

Visitor Transportation System

From Memorial Day through Labor Day, the visitor transportation system (VTS) operates a shuttle-bus service that provides regularly scheduled rides (for a fee) westward from the park's main visitor center to Toklat at Mile 53 (a six-hour round-trip); to Eielson Visitor Center at Mile 66 (an eight-hour round-trip); or all the way to Wonder Lake at Mile 85 (an 11-hour round-trip). During that period, visitors with cars may drive only to Savage River, 14.8 miles inside the park boundary. Presently only some of the space on the VTS is for reservations and the remaining seats are available on a first-come, first-served basis. Coupons may be obtained at the visitor access center up to two days in advance. Seats are in heavy

demand, so waits of up to two days are normal during peak season.

Buses make stops for wildlife viewing and at comfort stations. You may get off the bus along the park road except in closed areas for day hiking and catch a later bus back to the park entrance or campgrounds within the park. There is no food service on the buses, at the visitor centers, or comfort stations, so be sure to bring food, drink, warm clothes, and rain gear. Binoculars are also useful for viewing the incredible scenery and wildlife. For Denali bus reservations call 1-800-622-7275.

Special camper buses are provided to take campers and their gear into the park (make reservations when you make campsite reservations or get your backcountry pass). The VTS also provides free shuttle buses between the Denali Park Hotel, train station, Horseshoe Lake trailhead, visitor access center, Riley Creek Campground, and some visitor services outside the park.

Visitor Centers

Denali Visitor Access Center, located at .5 miles inside the park along the park road: open daily late May through September. Shuttle-bus coupons, backcountry permits, campsite registration, information, interpretive exhibits, audiovisial programs, publications, maps, schedules, and storage lockers.

Eielson Visitor Center, located approximately 68 miles inside the park along the Eielson Bluffs and accessible only by the visitor transportation system: open late June to mid-September. Information, limited displays, publications, maps, and observation deck.

Facilities

McKinley Mercantile, located across from the train station on Park Road, sells groceries, firewood, white gas, and other supplies as well as gasoline and propane. Similar convenience store services are available just north of the park entrance. Full vehicle service is available in Healy. A post office is near the park entrance. The closest bank or ATM is in Fairbanks, 120 miles away.

▶ *Creek near Wonder Lake in Denali National Park and Preserve, Alaska*

Handicapped Accessibility

All restrooms, most tour and shuttle buses, the visitor access center, the wildlife tour, ARA Denali Park Hotels, park headquarters, and the Eielson Visitor Center are wheelchair-accessible. Accessible sites near accessible toilets are reserved for use by disabled persons at Riley Creek, Savage, Teklanika, and Wonder Lake campgrounds. Persons with a telecommunication device for the deaf (TYY) can call the park year-round at 907-683-9649. Large-print scripts for the orientation slide show and the Denali Wilderness Film are available.

Medical Services

The Healy Clinic, 14 miles away, is open weekdays from 9 a.m. to 5 p.m.. A physician's assistant and registered nurse are on call 24 hours a day. The nearest hospital is in Fairbanks, 120 miles away.

Pets

Pets are allowed on roadways and in campgrounds only and must be leashed or physically restrained at all times. They are prohibited on buses and trails or in the backcountry. Pets

must not be left unattended. Please dispose of feces in garbage cans.

Climate

Denali's weather is characterized mostly by unpredictability. Visitors are cautioned to be prepared for sudden changes and all types of conditions.

Worship Services

Interdenominational services are held at the Denali Park Hotel Auditorium on Sundays at 9 a.m. and at Riley Creek Campground campfire

▲ *Dall sheep on a ridgeline in Denali National Park and Preserve, Alaska*

circle near site 27 at 6:30 p.m.. Catholic services are held on Saturdays at 5 p.m. at the same auditorium. Services are also available in Healy and Cantwell.

Safety and Regulations

For your safety and enjoyment and for the protection of the park, please follow these regulations and suggestions:

	AVERAGE DAILY	
Month	**Temperature F**	**Precipitation**
January	-7–11°	0.8 inches
February	-4–24°	0.6 inches
March	1–38°	0.5 inches
April	16–53°	0.5 inches
May	30–64°	0.8 inches
June	40–66°	2.3 inches
July	43–62°	3.8 inches
August	40–51°	2.6 inches
September	31–34°	1.5 inches
October	16–34°	1.0 inches
November	1–19°	0.8 inches
December	-6–11°	0.8 inches

- Motorized craft, including snowmobiles and ATVs, are prohibited in the Denali wilderness.

- Firearms must be unloaded, cased, and stored out of view; they should be left at park headquarters when you are backpacking in the wilderness area. Firearms are allowed in the preserve and park additions only.

- Some areas of the park and preserve may be temporarily closed because of wildlife activity. Entering closed areas is prohibited.

- While you are camping, all food must be stored in bear-resistant containers, available for free with a backcountry permit.

ACTIVITIES

Free naturalist-led activities include talks, walks, dogsled demonstrations, campground programs, and auditorium programs. Other activities include hiking, wildlife watching, mountain climbing, bus tours, cross-country skiing, snowshoeing, dogsledding, narrated wildlife bus tours, and rafting just outside the park entrance. Facilities in the park usually operate from late spring to early fall. Further information on activities, safety precautions, and a hiker's checklist are available in the park's newspaper, *Denali Alpenglow*.

Bus Tours

Bus tours run by the park concessioner are guided and provide either snacks or box lunches for a price depending on the length of the tour. There are departures throughout the day. Tours include the Denali Natural History Tour for 2.5 to three hours with a turnaround at mile 17, Primrose Ridge, and the Wildlife Tour for six to seven hours with a turnaround at mile 53, Toklat. On days good for viewing Denali, some trips may go as far as Stony Hill. In May and September, shortened trips into the park may be offered, depending upon weather and road conditions. Children under 12 years old ride at half price. Call 800-276-7234 for reservations.

Flightseeing

Small aircraft can be chartered for flight tours as well. A flight around the Alaska Range and Denali can be arranged through variety of operators at the park entrance or in Healy or Talkeetna.

Autumn Road Permit Lottery

The park operates an Autumn Road Lottery, allowing 1,600 private cars to drive the length of the park road. To apply for a permit, which is then selected by lottery, submit your name, address, and choice of dates (contact the park for road opening dates) in order of preference, along with a self-addressed, stamped envelope to Road Lottery, Denali National Park, P.O. Box 9, Denali NP, AK 99755. Applications must be mailed between July 1 and 31; only one entry per person is accepted.

Mountaineering

All Mount McKinley and Mount Foraker climbers must register prior to beginning their ascent, and there is a $150 per person mountaineering fee. Groups heading for other peaks are also urged to register. Contact the Talkeetna Ranger Station (at P.O. Box 588, Talkeetna, AK 99676 or 907-733-2231) for more information and registration forms.

Hiking Trails

Denali offers exciting hikes for both novice and experienced hikers. The only maintained park trails, mostly short loops, are near the hotel. Excellent opportunities exist for day hiking from the park road, while the best routes for hiking off trails are along river bars or ridgetops. If traveling in a group, be sure to spread out so as to avoid concentrated impact in an area. Remember that glacial streams can

▲ *Dall sheep relaxing in Denali National Park and Preserve, Alaska*

be cold, swift, and dangerous to cross, so sturdy footwear, raingear, and extra food and water are essential. Check at the visitor access center for backcountry information and areas closed to hiking.

Among the many trails available are: **Taiga Loop Trail,** an easy 1.3-mile loop beginning at the Denali Park Hotel parking area and crossing Horseshoe Creek, with connections to Mount Healy Overlook and Horseshoe Lake; **Morino Loop Trail,** an easy 1.3-mile loop beginning and ending at the Denali Park Hotel parking area, following Hines Creek and looping around the campground; **Rock Creek Trail,** a moderate, 2.3-mile route between Denali Park Hotel and Rock Creek, near park headquarters; **Roadside Trail,** a moderate, 1.8-mile route along the park road between Denali Park Hotel and Rock Creek, near park headquarters; **Horseshoe Lake Trail,** a moderate, .75-mile, self-guided interpretive route beginning at Mile 0.9 on the park road near the railroad track crossing and leading to Horseshoe Lake; and **Mount Healy Overlook,** a fairly strenuous, 2.5-mile route; beginning at the Denali Park Hotel parking area and following the Taiga Loop Trail for .3-mile to the start of the Mount Healy Overlook Trail after crossing the second service road. The first two-mile stretch of this trail is moderate.

OVERNIGHT STAYS

Lodging and Dining

Options include:

Denali Park Hotel, located one mile inside the park entrance, offers rooms from May through September, cafeteria, snack shop, lounge, and auditorium. For reservations, contact the hotel at P.O. Box 87, Denali National Park, AK 99755; 907-276-7234 or 907-683-2215. (This facility is scheduled to close by the year 2002.)

Denali National Park Wilderness Centers—North Face Lodge, located 89 miles inside the park, offers rooms, meals, and activities for about 36 people from early June to early September. Natural history, guided hiking emphasis. Bus accessible. For reservations, contact the lodge at P.O. Box 67, Denali National Park, AK 99755; 907-683-2290.

Denali National Park Wilderness Centers—Camp Denali, located 90 miles inside the park, offers cabins, meals, and activi-

ties for about 38 people from early June to early September. Natural history, guided hiking, special emphasis sessions on natural science, the environment, and nature photography. College credit field courses in northern studies. Bus accessible. For reservations, see address for North Face Lodge.

Kantishna Roadhouse, located 92 miles inside the park, offers cabins and rooms, meals, and activities for about 75 people from early June to early September. For reservations, contact the roadhouse at P.O. Box 81670, Fairbanks, AK 99708; 800-942-7420.

Denali Backcountry Lodge, located 94 miles inside the park, offers cabin-like rooms, meals, and activities from early June to early September. Bus accessible. For reservations, contact the lodge at P.O. Box 189, Denali National Park, AK 99755; 907-683-2594 or 800-841-0692.

Camping

Campers should register for campsites at the visitor access center (except for Morino, which has a self-registration system) and plan on camping outside the park when you first arrive, as there is often a two-night wait for campsites. There is a $4 one-time processing fee for phone or in-person reservations. The limit of stay during the season is 15 days; after Labor Day the limit of stay is 30 days. Water and flush toilets are available until early September. Trailers and motor homes are prohibited beyond Teklanika River. Morino, Sanctuary, Igloo, and Wonder Lake campgrounds are for tent camping only and require access by the visitor transport system or by walking to Morino. Private vehicle access is permitted to Teklanika Campground with a minimum three-night stay; road passes are good for only one trip to and from the campground during your stay, so bring all necessary items with you. Group camping is available at Savage River; reservations are required and can be made by writing Group Campground Reservations, Box 9, Denali National Park, AK 99755-0009 or calling 1-800-622-7275. There are three sites that accommodate 9-20 persons and two vehicles.

▶ *Rainbow at sunset reflected in pond near Wonder Lake in Denali National Park and Preserve, Alaska*

Campers are reminded to keep a clean camp and store food away to avoid attracting grizzly bears and other wildlife. Food must be kept in locked vehicles or storage lockers that are provided in all campgrounds. Fires are allowed only in established firepits; firewood can be purchased at McKinley Mercantile.

Backcountry Camping

Limited numbers of backcountry campers are permitted throughout most of the park. A backcountry permit is required and may be obtained in person one day in advance at the visitor access center. Campers should store food in bear-resistant containers, which the park issues with backcountry permits. Campfires are not permitted in Denali Wilderness. White gas is available at the McKinley Mercantile for cooking stoves. Campers should boil or treat all water; pack clothes, sleeping bag, and emergency gear in plastic bags to protect them during rainstorms and river crossings; and be thoroughly informed about wilderness and bear country safety.

FLORA AND FAUNA (Partial Listings)

Mammals: grizzly and black bears, barren ground caribou, moose, Dall sheep, lynx, gray wolf, coyote, red fox, wolverine, pine marten, mink, river otter, least and shorttail weasels, hoary marmot, beaver, porcupine, snowshoe hare, red and arctic ground squirrels, collared pika, and lemming.

Birds: loons (red-throated, Pacific, and common), red-necked grebe, trumpeter swan, green-winged teal, mallard, pintail, shoveler, American wigeon, harlequin duck, oldsquaw, common and Barrow's goldeneyes, bufflehead, common and red-breasted mergansers, osprey, goshawk, golden and bald eagles, peregrine falcon, gyrfalcon, ptarmigans (willow, rock, and white-tailed), grouse (spruce, ruffed, and sharp-tailed), golden plover, wandering tattler, sandpipers (solitary, spotted, and upland), whimbrel, surfbird, long-tailed jaeger, mew gull, arctic tern, owls (great horned, snowy, boreal, short-eared, and great gray), northern hawk-owl, belted kingfisher, woodpeckers (downy, hairy, three-toed, and black-backed), flicker, olive-sided and alder flycatchers, western wood pewee, Say's phoebe, horned lark, swallows (tree, violet-green, bank, and cliff), gray jay, black-billed magpie, raven, black-capped and boreal chickadees, dipper, ruby-crowned kinglet, thrushes (gray-cheeked, Swainson's, hermit, and varied), robin, wheatear, American pipit, Bohemian waxwing, warblers (orange-crowned, yellow, yellow-rumped or myrtle, blackpoll, and arctic), northern waterthrush, sparrows (tree, savannah, fox, Lincoln's, and white-crowned), lapland longspur, snow bunting, pine grosbeak, white-winged crossbill, and redpoll.

Trees, Shrubs, Flowers, and Berries: The season begins with the pasque flower, in early May. As spring progresses, a spectacular variety of sub arctic flowering plants can be seen in Denali, including woolly lousewart, alpine azalea, shootingstar, mountain avens, rock jasmine, and Scamman's spring beauty. The delicate arctic forget-me-not can be found in several alpine valleys in the park. During the course of the summer, these spring plants and others show their blossoms in areas where late melting snow begins to disappear. In mid-summer, river bars are covered with fireweed. Cotton grass, arnica, bearflower, and dwarf dogwood grace the tundra and taiga forests. Late summer and early autumn bring an abundance of wild berries such as blueberries, crowberries, and wild currants, combined with brilliant carpets of their autumn foliage color.

NEARBY POINTS OF INTEREST

The surrounding area offers many other outstanding natural attractions that can be enjoyed. Denali State Park is adjacent to the national park's southeastern boundary. The Denali Highway (State Route 8), formerly the main route to Denali running east from Cantwell just east of the park, is as popular for bicycling as is the park's main road. Tangle Lakes Archaeological District and Tetlin National Wildlife Refuge are also located to the east. About 50 miles north of Fairbanks is the White Mountains National Recreation Area.

GATES OF THE ARCTIC NATIONAL PARK AND PRESERVE

▲ Arrigetch Peaks reflecting in a pond

Gates of the Arctic National Park and Preserve

P.O. Box 26030
Bettles, AK 99726
907-692-5494

Gates of the Arctic, the second largest unit in the National Park System, contains diverse habitats that support an abundance of wildlife—notably the western arctic caribou herd, grizzly bears, moose, Dall sheep, and gray wolves. This 7,523,898-acre national park and adjacent 948,629-acre national preserve north of the Arctic Circle in north-central Alaska protect a vast, austere, uncompromising, yet awesomely beautiful wilderness of jagged-peaked mountain ranges, glacial cirques, high alpine meadows, treeless tundra, wooded lowlands, rugged canyons, pristine lakes, and numerous rivers and streams, including six national wild and scenic rivers. This utterly remote wilderness of unpeopled distances and unparalleled beauty was established by presidential proclamation as Gates of the Arctic National Monument in 1978. It was legislatively established as Gates of the Arctic National Park and Preserve in 1980 and was designated a Biosphere Reserve in 1984.

OUTSTANDING FEATURES

Among the many outstanding features of the park are the following: **Brooks Range,** the northwestern end of the Rocky Mountains and one of the world's northernmost mountain chains, which rises majestically from east-to-west for 180 miles through the heart of the park; **Boreal Mountain** and **Frigid Crags,** two precipitous peaks near the eastern end of the park, which like great portals boldly flank the North Fork of the Koyukuk River; these peaks were described in the early 1930s by pioneer wilderness-protection advocate and explorer Robert Marshall as the "Gates of the Arctic," opening northward through the Brooks Range and into the vast arctic tundra beyond; **Arrigetch Peaks,** a stunningly spectacular cluster of granite spires and saw-edged ridges in the southwestern part of the park; **Mount Igikpak,** the park's highest summit, rising to 8,510 feet elevation; **Alatna River,** a national wild and scenic river, providing a four- to seven-day wilderness float trip with a put-in either at Circle Lake and ending 85 miles to the south or at Takahula Lake and ending 75 miles to the south at the village of Allakaket; **John River,** a national wild and scenic river flowing southward through the heart of the park with a put-in at Hunt Fork Lake for a 100-mile wilderness float trip and ending south of the park at Bettles; **North Fork Koyukuk River,** a national wild and scenic river beginning at Summit Lake, flowing south through the Gates of the Arctic, and passing the Redstar Creek Lakes—a good put-in for a 100-mile float trip ending at Bettles; and **Noatak River,** a national wild and scenic river beginning its 450-mile course in the park, flowing through adjacent Noatak National Preserve, emptying into Chukchi Sea, and providing a month-long, 350-mile wilderness float trip from the put-in on Lake Matcharak to the village of Noatak.

PRACTICAL INFORMATION

When to Go

The park is open year-round. Summer is the most pleasant time of year, but weather is highly unpredictable all year and freezing temperatures can occur at any time. Summers are characteristically short, from June through July, with mild temperatures ranging from 50 to 80 degrees in lowland areas and 40 to 70 degrees in the highlands. The sun remains above the horizon 24 hours a day during these two months, during which time insects are a major concern. The winter season begins in August and is usually very rainy; autumn foliage colors peak in the middle of the month. Winters are long and cold, and most activity ceases, with the -20 to -50-degree temperatures that persist from November to March.

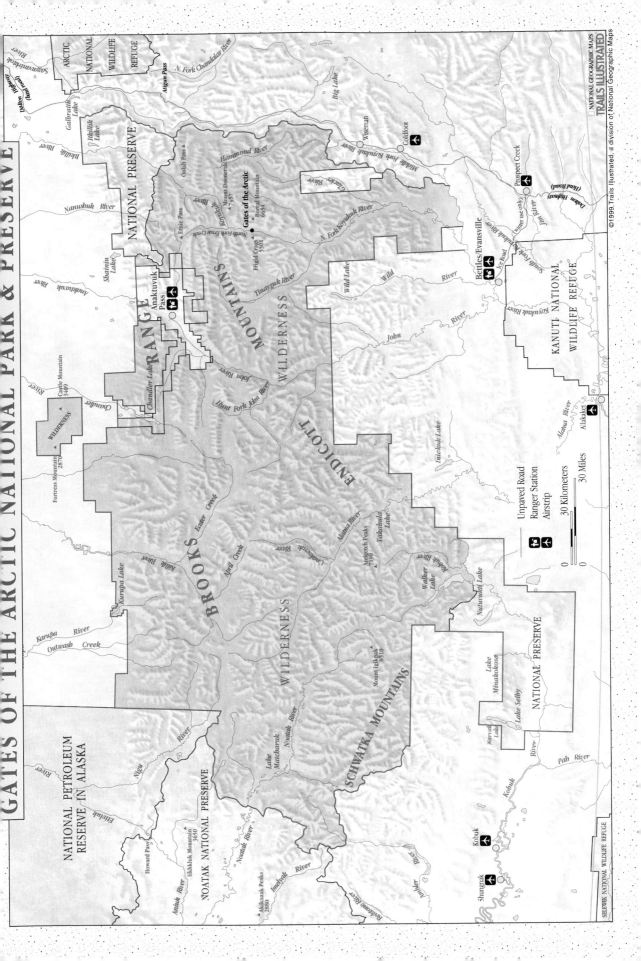

How to Get There

By Air: Fairbanks International Airport (907-474-2500) is the starting point for access to the park. Scheduled flights serve Bettles, Allakaket, and Anaktuvuk Pass. From those points or from Fairbanks, small aircraft can be chartered for flights into the park and preserve. Contact the park headquarters in Fairbanks for a list of licensed air taxis.

On Foot: Hiking or skiing into the park is possible by way of the Dalton Highway (pipeline haul road), but hazardous road conditions require special preparations. Some visitors hike in from the airfield at Anaktuvuk Pass. Contact a guide or air taxi operator to assist with planning, including information on access, landable sites, and other options.

Fees and Permits

There are no fees or permits for private parties, but commercial operators must have a valid commercial use license. An Alaska state fishing license is required. Sport hunting is prohibited in

the park, but permitted in the preserve in season with an Alaska hunting license.

▲ *Sunrise over Arrigetch Peaks in Gates of the Arctic National Park and Preserve, Alaska*

Ranger Stations

The only park ranger stations are at Bettles and Anaktuvuk Pass.

Facilities

No established trails, campgrounds, or other National Park Service facilities are provided in the park and preserve.

Handicapped Accessibility

Bettles, Anaktuvuk Pass, and Fairbanks ranger stations and rest rooms are wheelchair-accessible. Separate access or special assistance may be provided when access to existing programs is not reasonable or feasible, making most activities at ranger stations available for all visitors.

Options outside the park include:

Iniakuk Lake Wilderness Lodge, P.O. Box 80424, Fairbanks, AK 99708; 907-479-6354. Six rooms with shared bath and one cabin with private bath are available mid-June to mid-September.

Bettles Lodge (907-692-5111) offers rooms with shared baths and apartments with private baths. Open all year.

There are additional limited lodgings in Bettles, Anaktuvuk Pass, and Coldfoot. The Fairbanks Chamber of Commerce offers information.

Backcountry Camping

All camping is primitive and is allowed throughout the park. To protect fragile tundra environments, visitors are urged to camp on gravel bars or areas of hardy heath or moss vegetation. Check with rangers prior to camping to obtain current bear information. Obtain a topographic map prior to arrival since the park does not distribute detailed maps of the area.

FLORA AND FAUNA (Partial Listings)

Mammals: grizzly and black bears, barren ground caribou, Dall sheep, lynx, gray wolf, coyote, red and arctic foxes, wolverine, pine marten, mink, river otter, least and shorttail weasels, porcupine, hoary marmot, muskrat, snowshoe hare, arctic ground squirrel, and brown lemming.

Birds: loons (red-throated, Pacific, and common), geese (greater white-fronted, snow, and Canada), green-winged teal, mallard, wigeon, pintail, shoveler, greater and lesser scaups, harlequin duck, oldsquaw, surf and white-winged scoters, common and Barrow's goldeneye, bufflehead, red-breasted merganser, osprey, bald and golden eagles, northern harrier, goshawk, rough-legged hawk, merlin, peregrine falcon, gyrfalcon, grouse (spruce, ruffed, and sharp-tailed), willow and rock ptarmigans, sandhill crane, wandering tattler, golden plover, sandpipers (solitary, spotted, and upland), whimbrel, lesser yellowlegs, common snipe, red-necked phalarope, long-tailed jaeger, mew gull, arctic tern, owls (great horned, snowy, boreal, short-eared, and great gray), northern hawk-owl, belted kingfisher, three-toed woodpecker, flicker, olive-sided and alder flycatchers, Say's phoebe, swallows (tree, violet-green, bank, and cliff), gray jay, raven, black-capped and boreal chickadees, dipper, ruby-crowned kinglet, thrushes (gray-cheeked, Swainson's, and varied), robin, northern wheatear, American pipit, Bohemian waxwing, warblers (orange-crowned, yellow, yellow-rumped or myrtle, blackpoll, Wilson's, and arctic), northern waterthrush, sparrows (tree, savannah, fox, Lincoln's, golden-crowned, and white-crowned), dark-eyed junco, Lapland longspur, snow bunting, rosy finch, pine grosbeak, white-winged crossbill, and common and hoary redpolls.

Trees, Shrubs, and Flowers: white and black spruces, birches (paper, dwarf, and resin), quaking aspen, balsam poplar, Bebb willow, alders, Lapland rosebay, Labrador tea, bog rosemary, alpine azalea, lowbush and highbush cranberries, alpine blueberry, gray leaf, prickly and tundra roses, wild potato, wild sweet pea, fireweed, chiming bells, wild iris, larkspur, lousewort, yellow oxyprope, wooly louse, yellow anemone, dryas, common mustard, yellow cress, saxifrage, glacier and mountain avens, arctic and common forget-me-nots, grass-of-parnassus, Alaska spirea, and Siberian aster.

NEARBY POINTS OF INTEREST

The surrounding area offers other natural attractions that can be enjoyed. The park, together with Noatak National Preserve adjoining Gates of the Arctic to the west and the Kobuk Valley National Park adjoining Noatak, comprises one of the largest parkland areas in the world. To the south of the park is Kanuti National Wildlife Refuge, and to the west are Cape Krusenstern National Monument and Bering Land Bridge National Preserve, both on Alaska's west coast bordering Kotzebue Sound.

Glacier Bay National Park and Preserve

▲ *Icebergs and McBride Glacier*

GLACIER BAY NATIONAL PARK AND PRESERVE

P.O. Box 140
Gustavus, AK 99826-0140
907-697-2230

This 3,224,794-acre national park and adjacent 58,406-acre national preserve on the coast of southeastern Alaska protect a magnificently scenic area of snow- and ice-covered mountain peaks, nine narrow fjords, many bays and harbors, scattered coastal islands and rocks, a lush temperate rainforest of spruces and hemlocks, and numerous glaciers, a number of which extend to tide-water. During at least the past two centuries, the glaciers here, as elsewhere in the world, have been mostly melting and retreating—exposing vast expanses of rock and soil to the invasion of plantlife. This process of plant succession in the wake of retreating ice is clearly visible to visitors traveling northward up Glacier Bay by boat. Mature, dense conifer forest growing around Bartlett Bay, near the bay's mouth, gradually becomes thinner and the trees smaller until there are only thickets of vegetation. Still farther north, low-growing shrubs cover the otherwise barren ground until finally there is only bare rock and soil. The unusually rapid retreat of glacial ice at Glacier Bay—shrinking back roughly 65 miles in just 200 years—has provided geologists, botanists, and other researchers with unique opportunities to study the dynamics of glaciation and the successional invasion and re-establishment of plants and animals.

The park's varied habitats also support a tremendous diversity of wildlife, notably large colonies of nesting seabirds, great numbers of migrating ducks and geese, and such marine mammals as whales, porpoises, sea lions, and seals. Glacier Bay was established as a national monument by presidential proclamation in 1925; was legislatively established as a national park and preserve in 1980; and was designated a Biosphere Reserve in 1986.

OUTSTANDING FEATURES

Among the many outstanding features of the park are the following: **Muir Glacier,** a spectacular glacier that extends to tidewater and "calves" enormous chunks of ice into the bay; **Muir Inlet,** a mecca for kayakers because of its limited boat traffic and good opportunities for camping and hiking; **Mount Fairweather,** at 15,300 feet above sea level, the highest peak in southeast Alaska; **Alsek River,** a portion of which is protected within the park; and **Johns Hopkins Inlet,** the wildest fjord in the park, surrounded by peaks rising more than 6,000 feet.

PRACTICAL INFORMATION

When to Go

The main visitor season is from mid-May to mid-September, but the park is open year-round. Summer days are long, with temperatures usually around 45 degrees during the day and possibly going down to freezing at night. May and June usually have the most sunny days, but ice can still be quite thick then, making glaciers less approachable. Long periods of rainy, overcast, and cool weather are normal in southeast Alaska.

How to Get There

By Air: There are regularly scheduled commercial flights from Juneau International Airport (907-789-7821) to Gustavus, where transportation to tidewater glaciers can be arranged. Bus service from Gustavus to Bartlett Cove is available for those arriving on scheduled flights.

By Boat: The Alaska Marine Highway System (800-642-0066) serves Juneau, where boats can be chartered. Both cruise ships and smaller vessels take day and overnight trips to the Glacier Bay.

In addition, many guided trips are organized by private concessioners, which provide transportation to and in the park and preserve, including kayaking, backpacking, rafting, fish-

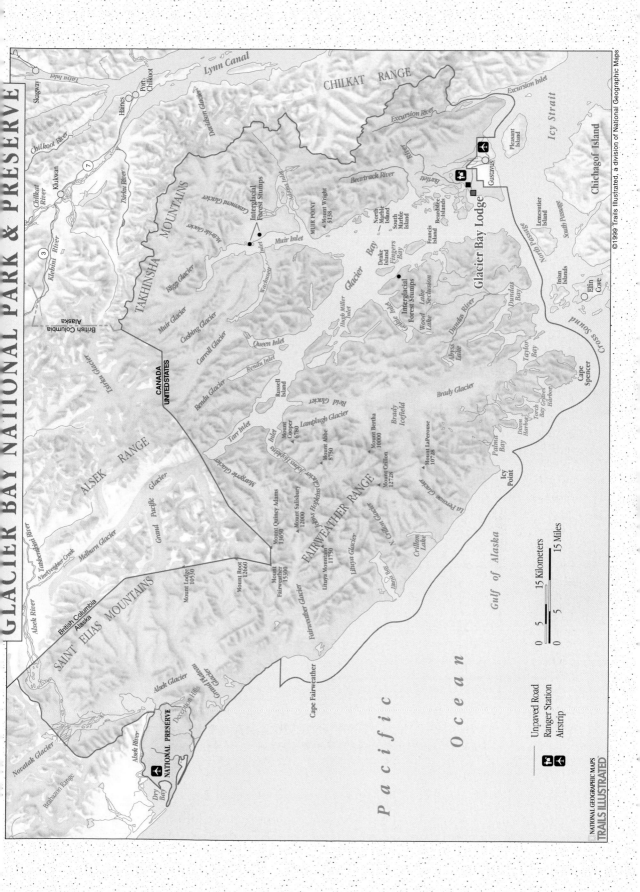

GLACIER BAY NATIONAL PARK & PRESERVE

NATIONAL GEOGRAPHIC MAPS
TRAILS ILLUSTRATED

Unpaved Road
Ranger Station
Airstrip

▲ *McBride Glacier in Glacier Bay National Park and Preserve, Alaska*

ing, and public hunting. Contact the park or the Juneau Chamber of Commerce for a complete listing.

Fees and Permits

There is no entrance fee, but fees are charged by private operators for transportation. Permits are required for private boaters from June 1 through August, and can be obtained by contacting the park by mail, phone, or VHF radio (KWM 20 BARTLETT COVE). Fishing and public hunting require state licenses.

Visitor Center and Ranger Station

Bartlett Cove Ranger Station offers information on the park/preserve. The dock has wayside exhibits, highlighting marine and natural history and the Tlingit Indian culture.

Glacier Bay Lodge has a visitor center upstairs, providing information, an interpretive sales area, and an auditorium for interpretive slide shows, films, and other programs.

Facilities

Limited facilities operating from mid-May through September include a lodge, restaurants, hot showers, laundry, and stores offering groceries, fuel, and firewood.

Handicapped Accessibility

In Glacier Bay Lodge, two of the rooms, as well as the restaurant, visitor center, auditorium, giftshop, book sales area, verandas, and public rest rooms are fully accessible via ramp or elevator. About 800 feet of accessible boardwalk winds through the local rainforest and culminates at viewing platforms. A videotaped introduction to the park in American Sign Language is available.

Medical Services

First aid is available at Bartlett Cove. The nearest hospital is in Juneau, 100 miles away.

Pets

Pets must be leashed or otherwise physically restrained at all times, and are only permitted in Bartlett Cove and on roads and trails. They are not permitted in the backcountry. Pets on boats must stay on board.

Safety and Regulations

For your safety and enjoyment and for the protection of the park, please follow these regulations and suggestions:

- Know what hypothermia is and how to guard against it.

- Grizzly (brown) and black bears are prevalent and should be considered potentially dangerous. When hiking, watch for bears and bear signs, make noise, travel in groups, and avoid night travel. Avoid taking odorous foods, prepare foods away from campsites, and use required bear-resistant food containers (available on loan). Hikers and campers should be thoroughly informed about guidelines for traveling in bear country.

- Prepare for biting insects.

- Boil or treat all water.

- Water craft must stay at least one quarter mile from tidewater glaciers and give a wide berth to icebergs since they frequently turn over or split apart and can be much larger than they appear above the surface.

- Remember that it is unlawful to destroy, injure, disturb, or remove any natural or cultural features or to feed, harass, capture, or kill wildlife.

- Firearms are prohibited in the park and can be secured at Bartlett Cove for the duration of your stay.

ACTIVITIES

Options include interpretive nature walks, films, slide presentations, evening programs, boat tours (either on charters or the lodge's *Spirit of Adventure*), kayaking, canoeing, fishing (license required), whale-watching, birdwatching, hiking, and mountain and glacier climbing (for experienced climbers only).

Hiking Trails

Among the available trails are: **Forest Loop**

Trail, an easy one-mile loop beginning and ending at Glacier Bay Lodge and leading through an area of lush, temperate rainforest of spruces and hemlocks; and **Bartlett River Trail,** an easy 1.5-mile route beginning on the road a half-mile from the lodge and leading through the rainforest to Bartlett River.

OVERNIGHT STAYS

Lodging and Dining

Inside the park, there is *Glacier Bay Lodge* (at Gustavus, AK 99826; 800-451-5952 or 907-697-2225) open from mid-May to mid-September offering rooms, restaurant, visitor center, films, slide shows, exhibits, fishing licenses, and guided tours. Reservations can be made off season by contacting Glacier Bay Lodge, Inc., 520 Pike St., Suite 1400, Seattle, WA 98101; 800-451-5952.

Outside the park, other lodging and meals are available in Gustavus. For a lodging brochure, write the Gustavus Visitors Association, P.O. Box 167, Gustavus, AK 99826.

Camping

Campers should attend the camper orientation program given twice daily at park headquarters. Bartlett Cove Campground is free and has bear-resistant food containers, firewood, and a warming hut. It operates on a first-come, first-served basis with a 14-day limit. Hot showers, laundry, drinking water, a restaurant, and white gas are available within a mile. Group camping is available all year on a first-come, first-served basis for groups of up to 20 people.

Backcountry Camping

Most backcountry use is done by kayak, with camping on beaches. Hiking inland is difficult because of steep terrain and dense vegetation. Backcountry camping is available all year on a first-come, first-served basis; registration at Bartlett Cove before departure is requested. Access generally requires drop-off by tour boat or float plane. There are no backcountry trails, but beaches, recently delegated areas, and alpine meadows offer

excellent hiking. Campers should be self-sufficient and fully equipped and provisioned. Cook stoves are necessary as wood is scarce and often wet; campfires are permitted only below the high tide line.

FLORA AND FAUNA (Partial Listings)

Mammals: Alaskan brown and black bears; moose; mountain goat; lynx; gray wolf; coyote; red fox; wolverine; pine marten; mink; river otter; least and shorttail weasels; hoary marmot; porcupine; red squirrel; harbor and northern fur seals; Steller sea lion; harbor porpoise; and humpback, minke (little piked), and killer (orca) whales.

Birds: loons (red-throated, Pacific, yellow-billed, and common), red-necked grebe, great blue heron, trumpeter swan, Canada goose, pelagic cormorant, green-winged and blue-winged teals, mallard, pintail, shoveler, gadwall, wigeon, greater scaup, harlequin duck, oldsquaw, scoters (black, surf, and white-winged), common and Barrow's goldeneyes, bufflehead, common and red-breasted mergansers, bald eagle, northern harrier, sharp-shinned hawk, goshawk, merlin, peregrine falcon, gyrfalcon, ptarmigan (willow, rock, and white-tailed), semipalmated plover, black oystercatcher, spotted sandpiper, common snipe, red-necked phalarope, gulls (mew, herring, and glaucous-winged), black-legged kittiwake, arctic tern, common murre, pigeon and black guillemots, murrelets (marbled, ancient, and Kittlitz's), tufted and horned puffins, owls (western screech, great horned, snowy, boreal, great gray, short-eared, and northern saw-whet), rufous hummingbird, woodpeckers (downy, hairy, and three-toed), flicker, olive-sided and alder flycatchers, horned lark, swallows (tree, violet-green, bank, and barn), Steller's jay, black-billed magpie, northwestern crow, raven, black-capped and chestnut-backed chickadees, red-breasted nuthatch, brown creeper, winter wren, dipper, golden-crowned and ruby-crowned kinglets, thrushes (gray-cheeked, Swainson's, hermit, and varied), robin, American pipit, Bohemian waxwing, warblers (orange-crowned, yellow, yellow-rumped or myrtle, and Wilson's), sparrows (tree, savan-

49

nah, fox, song, Lincoln's, golden-crowned, and white-crowned), dark-eyed junco, snow bunting, rosy finch, pine grosbeak, red and white-winged crossbills, and redpoll.

Trees, Shrubs, and Flowers: lodgepole pine, Sitka spruce, western hemlock, Alaska cedar, black cottonwood, willows, Sitka alder, skunk cabbage, devil's club,

51

▲ *Mount Fairweather and the Grand Plateau Glacier in Glacier Bay National Park and Preserve, Alaska*

salmonberry, bearberry, bog cranberry, blueberry, fireweed, lupine, mountain harebell, western columbine, chocolate lily, shootingstar, monkshood, paintbrushes, spring beauty, mountain avens, yellow violet, bunchberry, buttercup, bog orchid, moss campion, purple mountain saxifrage, bell heather, and Siberian aster.

▲ *Rafters in Alsek Lake, Glacier Bay National Park and Preserve, Alaska*

NEARBY POINTS OF INTEREST

The surrounding area offers other natural and historical attractions that can be enjoyed. Adjoining the park are the Tongass National Forest and Canada's Tatshenshini-Alsek Wilderness Provincial Park. Nearby, to the northeast, is Klondike Gold Rush National Historical Park in and near Skagway. To the south are Sitka National Historical Park on Baranof Island and two U.S. Forest Service-managed areas: Admiralty Island National Monument south of Juneau and Misty Fjords National Monument near Ketchikan. To the northwest are Wrangell-St. Elias National Park and Preserve and Canada's adjoining Kluane National Park.

Katmai National Park and Preserve

▲ *The River Lethe*

Katmai National Park and Preserve

**P.O. Box 7
King Salmon, AK 99613-0007
907-246-3305**

This 3,674,540-acre national park and adjacent 418,699-acre national preserve located at the northern end of the Alaska Peninsula in southwest Alaska protects an extensive, partly active volcanic field with 15 active volcanoes, stretching along the rugged coast of Shelikof Strait. Inland, the park encompasses a vast wilderness of lakes, marshes, rivers, waterfalls, and the edge of coniferous forest. This area provides valuable habitat for an abundance of fish and wildlife, notably the sockeye (red) salmon and the state's highest population density of the Alaskan brown bear—North America's largest carnivorous mammal.

Katmai was initially established in 1918 by presidential proclamation as a national monument, following the cataclysmic volcanic eruption of Novarupta Volcano in 1912—one of the three most powerful volcanic explosions ever recorded in the world. Estimated to have had ten times the force of the 1980 eruption of Mount St. Helens in Washington State, Novarupta ejected enormous quantities of glowing pumice and ash, burying more than 40 square miles of surrounding land beneath as much as 700 feet of the volcano's deposits and darkening the sky around most of the Northern Hemisphere with volcanic dust. In 1931, the monument was expanded to the northwest to protect a major area of Alaskan brown bear habitat, and a number of coastal islands were added in 1942. In 1980, the area was further enlarged and legislatively established as a national park and preserve.

OUTSTANDING FEATURES

Among the many outstanding features of the park are the following: **Novarupta Volcano,** from which it is believed most of the lava and ash exploded in the gigantic eruption in 1912; **Mount Katmai caldera,** containing a "robin's-egg blue" crater lake where there was formerly a huge volcano, the summit of which collapsed as Novarupta's eruption was believed to have drained off magma from within once-massive Mount Katmai; the **Valley of Ten Thousand Smokes,** an area named for the countless fumaroles that continued to steam 500-to-1,000 feet into the air for many years after the 1912 eruption; **Three Forks Overlook,** a spot offering visitors a view of the Valley of Ten Thousand Smokes; **Ukak River** (near Three Forks Overlook), which plunges through a deep gorge topped by cliffs of volcanic ash; **Brooks Falls,** a six-foot-high waterfall where visitors—especially in July—can watch Alaskan brown bears fishing for leaping sockeye salmon, which migrate from the ocean to the headwaters of the Naknek system of rivers and lakes to spawn in August, September, and October; and the **Bay of Islands,** an especially beautiful part of the North Arm of the park's largest lake, Naknek.

PRACTICAL INFORMATION

When to Go

The park is open year-round, but the main visitor season runs from June to early September, when concessions, transportation operations, lodging, and camping facilities are open. The salmon migrate in July, making it prime bear-watching time. Early September is also very good for bear viewing. Summer daytime temperatures range from 55 to 65 degrees, with the average low at 44 degrees. Strong winds and sudden gusts frequently sweep the area. Skies are clear about 20 percent of the summer, and light rain can last for days.

How to Get There

By Air: Anchorage International Airport (907-266-2437) has daily commercial flights (weather permitting) to King Salmon, about six miles west of the park boundary. Commercial float planes operate daily from King Salmon and Brooks Camp from June to September. Year-

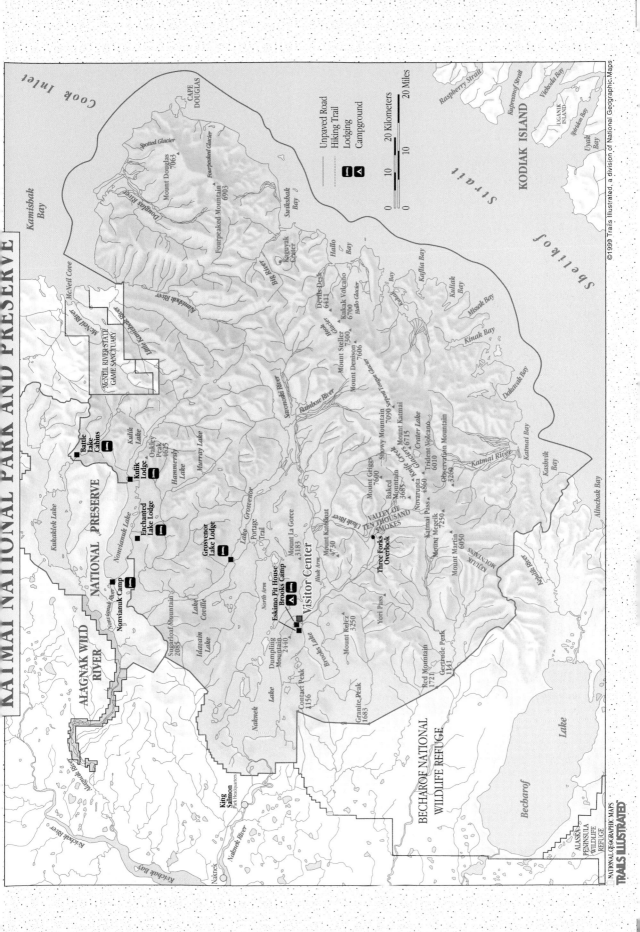

KATMAI NATIONAL PARK AND PRESERVE

Cook Inlet

Shelikof Strait

KODIAK ISLAND

Raspberry Strait

Kupreanof Strait

UGANIK ISLAND

Spiridon Bay

Viekoda Bay

Uyak Bay

CAPE DOUGLAS

Spotted Glacier

Fourpeaked Glacier

Mount Douglas 7063

Fourpeaked Mountain 6903

Kamishak Bay

Swikshak Bay

McNeil Cove

Douglas River

Kaguyak Glacier

Hallo Bay

Devils Desk 6411

Kukak Volcano 6700

Hallo Glacier

Kukak Bay

Kaflia Bay

Missak Bay

Kinak Bay

Dakavak Bay

McNEIL RIVER STATE GAME SANCTUARY

McNeil River

Little Kamishak River

Kamishak River

Big River

Savonoski River

Soluka Creek

Rainbow River

Serpent Tongue Glacier

Mount Steller 7300

Mount Denison 7606

Snowy Mountain 7090

Mount Katmai 6715

Crater Lake

Trident Volcano 6010

Observation Mountain 3269

Katmai River

Kukaklek Lake

NATIONAL PRESERVE

ALAGNAK WILD RIVER

Battle Lake Cabins

Kulik Lake

Kulik Lodge

Oakley Peak 4625

Hammersly Lake

Murray Lake

Nonvianuk Lake

Enchanted Lake Lodge

Grosvenor Lake Lodge

Lake Grosvenor

Nonvianuk River

Nonvianuk Camp

Sugarloaf Mountain 2085

Lake Coville

Idavain Lake

Mount La Gorce 3183

Lake Portage Trail

North Arm

Iliuk Arm

Mount Katolinat 4730

Ukak River

Baked Mountain 3685

Novarupta 4860

Mageik 7250

Mount Mageik 7250

VALLEY OF TEN THOUSAND SMOKES

Three Forks Overlook

Katmai Pass

Mount Griggs 7600

Mount Martin 6050

Kashvik Bay

Katmai Bay

KEJULIK MOUNTAINS

Eskimo Pit House
Brooks Camp
Visitor Center

Dumpling Mountain 2440

Brooks Lake

Mount Kelez 3250

Yori Pass

Red Mountain 1721

Gertrude Peak 1141

Contact Peak 4156

Granite Peak 1683

Naknek Lake

King Salmon
Park Headquarters

Naknek

Naknek River

Kvichak River

Kvichak Bay

BECHAROF NATIONAL WILDLIFE REFUGE

Becharof Lake

Egegik River

ALASKA PENINSULA WILDLIFE REFUGE

Unpaved Road
Hiking Trail
Lodging
Campground

20 Miles
20 Kilometers
10
10
0
0

NATIONAL GEOGRAPHIC MAPS
TRAILS ILLUSTRATED

©1999 Trails Illustrated, a division of National Geographic Maps

round air charter services are available in King Salmon. The park provides a list of operators.

By Boat: Commercial operators provide access to King Salmon and the Brooks River via special boats.

Fees and Permits

There are no entrance fees. Transportation to, from, and within the park is by private, fee-charging concessioners. Public hunting is permitted only in the national preserve. Fishing licenses are required and all state rules apply. Permits for backcountry travel are recommended and can be obtained at the Brooks Camp Visitor Center or at park headquarters in King Salmon.

Visitor Center

Brooks Camp Visitor Center: open June through mid-September. Information, interpretive programs, maps, and publications.

Facilities and Services

The following are available from June to mid-September: bear-viewing platform at Brooks Falls, restaurant, camp store, hot showers, canoe and kayak rentals, white gas, fishing tackle, and bookstore.

Handicapped Accessibility

Most trails at Brooks Camp and the bear-viewing platforms on the Brooks River are accessible.

Medical Services

Only limited first aid is available in the park, but a clinic in Naknek, about 15 miles west of park headquarters, has a doctor on duty during the summer. The nearest hospital is in Anchorage.

Pets

Pets are permitted only on private vessels and within one mile of the Naknek River. Check with the park for more information.

Safety and Regulations

For your safety and enjoyment and for the protection of the park, please follow these regulations and suggestions:

- All visitors to Katmai must proceed to the contact station for an orientation program on bear encounters, proper behavior around bears, and information on current bear activity.

- Be well prepared at all times for encounters with bears including around developed facilities and be prepared for rugged wilderness conditions. Gear must be able to withstand blowing rain and high winds of up to 50-60 mph.

- Know what hypothermia is and how to deal with it.

- Be prepared to wait out storms, carry matches, first-aid kit, and emergency food.

- Be extremely cautious when crossing streams, and especially muddy waters.

- When boating, stay close to shore, and watch carefully for rapidly changing weather conditions.

- Hunting or discharging any weapon is prohibited in the park, and firearms must be unloaded and cased.

- It is important to remember that bears, moose, and other animals are unpredictable

▲ *Paddling Naknek Lake in Katmai National Park and Preserve, Alaska*

and can be dangerous. Visitors are urged to read and study the park pamphlet about bears and to ask rangers about special precautions for backcountry camping, fishing, camping, and hiking. Do not fish near bears. When you catch a fish, avoid attracting bears by immediately putting it in a plastic bag and taking it immediately to the fish-cleaning house. Practicing safety precautions in bear country is essential.

▲ *Grizzly bear fishing at Brooks Falls in Katmai National Park and Preserve, Alaska*

ACTIVITIES

Options include hiking, kayaking, canoeing, boating, boat tours, mountain climbing, fishing (license required), float trips, interpretive programs, bear and other wildlife watching, guided canoe trips, guided backpacking trips, guided fishing trips, van tours, and guided walks. Further information is available in the park's publication, *Bear Facts*.

Hiking Trails

Trails in the Brooks Camp vicinity include: **Brooks Falls Trail,** an easy half-mile route beginning at Brooks Camp and ending on the Brooks Falls bear-viewing platform;

Dumpling Mountain Trail, a moderate, 1.5-mile route beginning at Brooks Camp campground and climbing to an 800-foot-high overlook, affording a view (weather permitting) of Naknek Lake. An additional two-mile hike leads across tundra to the 2,440-foot summit of Dumpling Mountain, from which is a broad panorama (weather permitting) of Naknek Lake.

Trails in the Valley of Ten Thousand Smokes vicinity include: **Three Forks Overlook-to-Ukak River Trail,** a short, 200-foot descent for a view of the Ukak River dashing through a gorge, the cliffs of which are composed of layers of volcanic ash;

Baked Mountain Cabin Trail, a strenuous, 12-mile trek beginning near the end of the Brooks Camp-to-Three-Forks Overlook Road, crossing Windy Creek, following the River Lethe, and climbing 1,000 feet to this overnight cabin. Midway between the cabin and Katmai Pass, hikers can branch off to Novarupta, the volcanic plug (dome) from which it is believed that most of the pumice and ash exploded in 1912.

OVERNIGHT STAYS

Lodging and Dining

Katmailand, Inc., offers package tours from Anchorage that include airfare, lodging, meals, guides, rafts, licenses, fishing tackle, and transportation to fishing spots. They can be contacted at 4550 Aircraft Drive, Suite 2, Anchorage, AK 99502; 907-243-5448; 800-544-0551, for reservations and more information on the following three lodges: *Brooks Lodge,* open June to mid-September, offering cabins, dining room, bar service, and tours;

Grosvenor Lodge, between Grosvenor and Coville lakes, open June to late September, offering cabins, dining room, bar service, and guided trips; and *Kulik Lodge,* on Nonvianuk Lake, open from mid-June to late September, offering cabins, dining room, bar service, and guided trips.

Other options include: *Enchanted Lake Lodge* (P.O. Box 97, King Salmon, AK 99613; 907-246-6878 May through September; 206-643-2172 October through April), on Nonvianuk Lake, open June to October; and *Battle River Wilderness Retreat* (8076 Caribbean Way, Sacramento, CA 95826; 916-381-0250) near Battle Lake, open July through September, offering cabins with central showers, meals, guided float fishing trips, and wildlife viewing.

Campgrounds

Brooks Camp Campground provides tent sites, water, pit toilets, food storage caches, fire pits, and picnic tables. It is open from May to early September by reservation only by contacting National Park Reservation Service at 800-365-CAMP. Three shelters for cooking are provided. Fires are permitted only in established fire pits or camp stoves.

Backcountry Camping

Permits are not required for backcountry camping, which can be done anywhere in the park outside of a two-mile corridor along the Brooks River. Contact the park for a free brochure, "Traveling the Katmai Backcountry." Food must be stored at least ten feet above ground or in approved bear-resistant containers. There are no improved campsites or food caches in the backcountry. Visitors are urged to follow minimum-impact camping guidelines and to be fully informed about traveling and camping safety in bear country.

FLORA AND FAUNA (Partial Listings)

Mammals: Alaskan brown and black bears, barren ground caribou, moose, lynx, gray wolf, red fox, wolverine, pine marten, mink, sea otter, river otter, least and shorttail weasels, porcupine, beaver, snowshoe hare, red squirrel, lemming, harbor seal, Steller sea lion, harbor porpoise, and killer (orca), beluga, and gray whales.

Birds: loons (red-throated, Pacific, and common), red-necked and horned grebes, cormorants (double-crested, pelagic, and red-faced), tundra and trumpeter swans, greater white-fronted and Canada geese, green-winged teal, mallard, pintail, gadwall, shoveler, greater scaup, eiders (common, king, and Steller's), harlequin duck, oldsquaw, scoters (black, surf, and white-winged), common and Barrow's goldeneyes, bufflehead, common and red-breasted mergansers, bald and golden eagles, northern harrier, rough-legged hawk, osprey, merlin, peregrine falcon, gyrfalcon, spruce grouse, willow and rock ptarmigan, sandhill crane, semipalmated plover, black oystercatcher, sandpipers (solitary, spotted, least, and rock), dunlin, short-billed dowitcher, greater yellowlegs, common snipe, red-necked phalarope, long-tailed and parasitic jaegers, gull (mew, herring, and glaucous-winged), black-legged kittiwake, arctic tern, common and thick-billed murres, pigeon guillemot, marbled and ancient murrelet, parakeet auklet, tufted and horned puffins, owls (great horned, snowy, and short-eared), belted kingfisher, three-toed woodpecker, flicker, olive-

▲ *The Valley of 10,000 Smokes in Katmai National Park and Preserve, Alaska*

sided flycatcher, Say's phoebe, horned lark, swallows (tree, violet-green, bank, and cliff), gray jay, black-billed magpie, northwestern crow, raven, black-capped chickadee, winter wren, dipper, thrushes (gray-cheeked, Swainson's, hermit, and varied), robin, northern wheatear, American pipit, warblers (orange-crowned, yellow, yellow-rumped or myrtle, blackpoll, and Wilson's), sparrows (tree, savannah, fox, Lincoln's, song, golden-crowned, and white-crowned), dark-eyed junco, lapland longspur, snow bunting, rosy finch, white-winged crossbill, pine grosbeak, and common redpoll.

Trees, Shrubs, and Flowers: Sitka and white spruces, paper and dwarf birches, balsam poplar, willows, alder, alpine blueberry, crowberry, Labrador tea, lowbush cranberry, fireweed, wild geranium, and alpine azalea.

NEARBY POINTS OF INTEREST

The surrounding area offers other exciting natural and historical attractions that can be enjoyed. Becharof National Wildlife Refuge adjoins the park to the southwest and Alaska Peninsula Wildlife Refuge adjoins the Becharof refuge. Alagnak Wild River adjoins the national preserve to the northwest. Aniakchak National Monument and Preserve are farther southwest on the Alaska Peninsula. Lake Clark National Park and Preserve are to the north. Kenai Fjords National Park and Preserve and Kachemak Bay State Park are to the northeast on the Kenai Peninsula. Fort Abercrombie State Historical Park is to the east across Shelikof Strait on Kodiak Island.

KENAI FJORDS NATIONAL PARK

▲ Sculpted ice cave

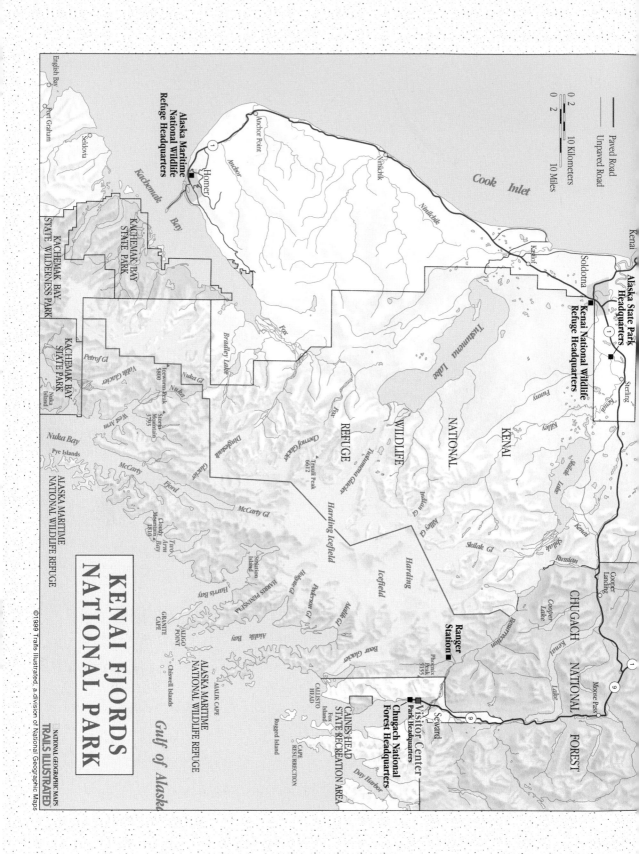

KENAI FJORDS NATIONAL PARK

Paved Road
Unpaved Road

0 2   10 Kilometers
0 2   10 Miles

Cook Inlet

Gulf of Alaska

English Bay
Port Graham
Seldovia
Kachemak Bay

KACHEMAK BAY
STATE
WILDERNESS PARK

KACHEMAK BAY
STATE PARK

KACHEMAK BAY
STATE PARK

Alaska Maritime
National Wildlife
Refuge Headquarters

Homer

Anchor Point
Anchor
Ninilchik
Ninilchik
Kasilof
Soldotna
Kenai

Alaska State Park
Headquarters

Kenai National Wildlife
Refuge Headquarters

Sterling
Funny
Skilak Lake
Skilak
Kenai
Russian
Cooper
Lake
Cooper
Landing
Moose Pass

CHUGACH
NATIONAL
FOREST

KENAI   NATIONAL   WILDLIFE   REFUGE

Tustumena Lake

Fox
Fox

Bradley Lake

Petrof Gl
Dixie Glacier
Nuka Gl
Iceworm Peak 5800
Storm Mountain 3795
West Arm
Nuka

Tustumena Glacier

Chernof Glacier
Truuli Peak 6612

Judson G.

Skilak Gl

Harding   Icefield

Harding Icefield

Glacier
Fjord

McCarty
McCarty Gl

Nuka Bay

Pye Islands

Cloudy
Mountain 4810
Tivo
Cloudy Arm Bay
Sheldon
Island
Holgate Gl
Paterson Gl
Pederson Gl

Harris Bay
HARRIS PENINSULA
Aialik Gl
Aialik Bay

NUKA POINT
GRANITE CAPE
AIALIK CAPE
Chiswell Islands
Rugged Island
Fox Island
CALLISTO HEAD
CAPE RESURRECTION
Day Harbor

Bear Glacier

Phoenix Peak 5155

Ranger Station

Resurrection

Seward

Visitor Center
Park Headquarters
Chugach National
Forest Headquarters

CAINES HEAD
STATE RECREATION AREA

CHUGACH

NATIONAL

FOREST

Nuka
Island

ALASKA MARITIME
NATIONAL WILDLIFE REFUGE

ALASKA MARITIME
NATIONAL WILDLIFE REFUGE

NATIONAL GEOGRAPHIC MAPS
TRAILS ILLUSTRATED

Kenai Fjords National Park

P.O. Box 1727
Seward, AK 99664-1727
907-224-3175

This national park along the southeastern coast of the Kenai Peninsula in southcentral Alaska protects scenic and pristine seascapes and landscapes of seven long fjords; towering, snow-covered mountains; narrow, glacier-filled valleys; a vast icefield; deep canyons; plunging waterfalls; and a rocky Gulf of Alaska coastline of endless bays, coves, and peninsulas, along which marine mammals and seabirds nest and raise their young. The 670,642-acre park was initially proclaimed a national monument in 1978 and was legislatively renamed a national park in 1980.

OUTSTANDING FEATURES

Among the many outstanding features of the park are the following: **Harding Ice Field,** the 700-square-mile mass of ice up to a mile thick, which annually receives roughly 30 feet of snow and feeds more than 30 glaciers; **Exit Glacier,** the most accessible and popular area of the park; **Aialik Bay,** a scenically spectacular and most heavily visited of the park's fjords—where Holgate, Pederson, and Aialik glaciers extend thousands of feet down from the Harding Icefield; **Harris Bay,** the second major fjord, located northeast-to-southwest, where Northwestern Glacier retreated nearly ten miles from 1910 to 1960; and **McCarty Fjord,** the third major, narrow, mountain-framed arm of the sea—extending 23 miles inland to the end of McCarty Glacier.

PRACTICAL INFORMATION

When to Go

The park is open year-round, but spring through summer is the best time to visit. The road to Exit Glacier is usually open from May until the first snowfall, probably in October. Overcast and/or cool days are the norm for summer in this maritime climate of abundant rainfall; warm sunny summer days are the welcome exception. May is the driest month; successive months thereafter generally bring increasing precipitation. By mid-June, daytime temperatures reach 55 to 65°. September initiates the wet and stormy autumn.

How to Get There

By Car: From Anchorage, take the spectacular 130-mile drive on Seward Highway (State Routes 1 and 9) to Seward—the gateway to the park.

By Air: Anchorage International Airport (907-266-2437) is served by major airlines. Commuter and charter flights are also available to Seward.

By Train: The Alaska Railroad (800-544-0552) serves Seward from Anchorage during the summer.

By Bus: Gray Line of Alaska (907-277-5581) serves Anchorage, from which there is bus service to Seward; Seward Bus Line (907-563-0800).

By Ferry: The Alaska Marine Highway System (800-642-0066) ferry service links Valdez, Seward, Kodiak, and Homer.

Fees and Permits

There are no park fees.

Visitor Center and Ranger Station

Kenai Fjords Visitor Center, in Seward: open daily in the summer and weekdays for the rest of the year. Information, interpretive exhibits, slide programs, maps, and publications.

Exit Glacier Ranger Station: open daily in the summer only. Interpretive exhibits on the glacier and the Harding Icefield, guided nature hikes, and evening programs.

Handicapped Accessibility

A half-mile trail from Exit Glacier Ranger Station provides handicapped access to within

▲ *Exit Glacier in Kenai Fjords National Park, Alaska*

a quarter mile of the glacier and has wayside nature exhibits. Also accessible are the visitor center and public use cabins.

Medical Services

First aid and a hospital are available in Seward, just outside the eastern boundary of the park.

Pets

Pets are permitted on leashes on the Exit Glacier Road and in parking areas. They are prohibited on all trails.

Safety and Regulations

For your safety and enjoyment and for the protection of the park, please follow these regulations and suggestions:

- Backcountry travel without a guide requires discussing plans, weather, etc., with a ranger.

- The Harding Icefield brings sudden storms, high winds, blinding sunlight, and extreme temperature changes.

- Know what hypothermia is and how to avoid and treat it.

- Discuss guidelines for traveling in bear country with a ranger.

- Never feed, disturb, or approach any wildlife.

- All federal and state boating regulations apply. A seaworthy craft and rough water boating experience are absolutely required. File a float plan with a responsible person.

ACTIVITIES

Options include guided boat tours, wildlife viewing, sea kayaking, sailing, hiking, camping, mountain climbing, fishing trips, bus tours, dogsledding, snowshoeing, day skiing on Harding Icefield, summer boat charters, air charters, bus tours to Exit Glacier, commercial guides for camping, and interpretive programs. Much of the coastline has been transferred to Alaska Native Corporations, which limits former use of coastal areas for camping. However, 30,000 acres of private coastline were acquired by the park in 1997 with NPCA's assitance and the National Park Service has negotiated easements that allow access to the public-use cabins. Visitors should check on access to specific areas. The Exit Glacier area, at the northeast end of the park, is one of the best places in Alaska to reach a

major glacier on foot. There is also trail access onto Harding Icefield, one of the world's largest. Further information is available in the park's newspaper, *The Nunatak.*

Hiking Trails

Trails in the Exit Glacier vicinity include: **Main Trail,** an easy, quarter-mile, paved path beginning at the Exit Glacier Ranger Station

▲ *Aerial view of Ariadne Island in Kenai Fjords National Park, Alaska*

and leading to a viewing area, then continuing another quarter-mile on a steeper stretch across bedrock and moraines to the terminus of Exit Glacier; **Nature Trail,** an easy half-mile, self-guided interpretive route, offering an alternative route back to the ranger station

◀ *Three Hole Point in Kenai Fjords National Park, Alaska*

through cottonwoods, alders, and willows and along Exit Creek; and **Harding Icefield Trail,** a fairly strenuous, three-mile climb, branching from the Main Trail and following the flank of the glacier to an overlook of the icefield. The National Park Service advises that visitors check bulletin boards for trail conditions, as heavy rains do result in closure of this route. Visitors are cautioned to stay off the ice, as this is an active glacier and "calving" poses hazards. Winter travel into the Exit Glacier area is by cross-country skiing, snowshoeing, and dogsledding.

OVERNIGHT STAYS

Lodging and Dining

There are no overnight accommodations or food services in the park. The gateway community of Seward provides a full range of visitor accommodations. Contact the Chamber of Commerce for more information.

Campgrounds and Cabins

Exit Glacier Campground, located in an alder and willow forest in the Resurrection River drainage a quarter mile from Exit Glacier, is open from late May to early October on a first-come, first-served basis and does not charge a fee. Ten sites, pit toilets, pumped water, and grills are provided. Public-use cabins are available for overnight lodging by reservation; cabin permits are required. Two are located on the shores of Aialik Bay, one at McCarty Fjord, one at the North Arm of Nuka Bay, and one at Exit Glacier (the latter for winter use only).

Backcountry Camping

Backcountry camping is allowed throughout the park. Permits are not required, but registration is requested for travel on the Harding Icefield. Be sure to be well informed about guidelines for traveling in bear country, keep a clean and odor-free campsite, and cook and store food well away from tents.

Mammals: Alaskan brown and black bears, mountain goat, barren ground caribou, lynx, gray wolf, coyote, red fox, wolverine, pine marten, mink, river otter, sea otter, least and shorttail weasels, hoary marmot, beaver, muskrat, snowshoe hare, arctic ground squirrel, red squirrel, harbor seal, dall and harbor porpoises, Steller sea lion, and killer (orca), minke, humpback, and gray whales.

Birds: loons (red-throated, Pacific, yellow-billed, and common), horned and red-necked grebes, cormorants (double-crested, red-faced, and pelagic), great blue heron, green-winged and blue-winged teals, mallard, pintail, shoveler, gadwall, wigeon, greater scaup, common and king eiders, harlequin duck, oldsquaw, scoters (black, surf, and white-winged), common and Barrow's goldeneyes, bufflehead, common and red-breasted mergansers, sooty and short-tailed shearwaters, bald and golden eagles, osprey, northern harrier, sharp-shinned hawk, goshawk, merlin, peregrine falcon, gyrfalcon, spruce grouse, ptarmigans (willow, rock, and white-tailed), semipalmated plover, black oystercatcher, greater yellowlegs, wandering tattler, sandpipers (spotted, least, and rock), common snipe, red-necked phalarope, parasitic jaeger, gulls (Bonaparte's, mew, herring, and glaucous-winged), black-legged kittiwake, arctic tern, common and thick-billed murres, pigeon guillemot, murrelets (marbled, ancient, and Kittlitz's), rhinoceros auklet, tufted and horned puffins, owls (great horned, snowy, boreal, great gray, northern saw-whet, and short-eared), northern hawk-owl, rufous hummingbird, belted kingfisher, woodpeckers (downy, hairy, and three-toed), olive-sided and alder flycatchers, horned lark, swallows (tree, violet-green, bank, and cliff), gray and Steller's jays, black-billed magpie, northwestern crow, raven, chickadees (black-capped, boreal, and chestnut-backed), red-breasted nuthatch, brown creeper, winter wren, dipper, golden-crowned and ruby-crowned kinglets, thrushes (gray-cheeked, Swainson's, hermit, and varied), robin, American pipit, Bohemian waxwing, warblers (orange-crowned, yellow, yellow-rumped or myrtle, Townsend's, blackpoll, and Wilson's), northern waterthrush, sparrows (savannah, fox, Lincoln's, golden-crowned, and white-crowned), dark-eyed junco, snow bunting, rosy finch, pine grosbeak, red and white-winged crossbills, and common redpoll.

Trees, Shrubs, and Flowers: Sitka spruce, western and mountain hemlocks, black cottonwood, willows, Sitka alder, devil's club, blueberry, salmonberry, fireweed, western columbine, bunchberry, forget-me-not, and lupine.

NEARBY POINTS OF INTEREST

The surrounding area offers other exciting natural attractions that can be enjoyed. Bordering the park are Kachemak Bay State Park and Kachemak Bay State Wilderness Park, Kenai National Wildlife Refuge, and Chugach National Forest. Caines Head State Recreation Area and the Alaska Maritime National Wildlife Refuge are nearby, the latter encompassing clusters of islands just offshore from the park.

WRANGELL–ST. ELIAS NATIONAL PARK AND PRESERVE

▲ Ice forms and Mount St. Elias

Wrangell–St. Elias National Park and Preserve

P.O. Box 439
Copper Center, AK 99573
907-822-5235

This national park and preserve along the Canadian border in southcentral Alaska are by far the largest National Park System unit and nearly six times the size of Yellowstone. The 8,323,617-acre national park and adjacent 4,852,773-acre national preserve protect an immense and scenically awesome wilderness in North America's largest concentration of peaks where three major mountain ranges converge, along with the world's highest coastal mountains—the St. Elias, which extend into Canada's adjacent 5,400,000-acre Kluane National Park.

Among the snow- and ice-covered summits, the park boasts nine of the 16 highest peaks in the United States, including the second highest. There are vast icefields, the largest stretching for 100 miles, along with plunging waterfalls, streams, and broad, braided rivers. More than 150 glaciers wind down from the heights, including the largest piedmont glacier in North America. Located mostly within the national preserve are three major vegetational areas—coastal coniferous, northern coniferous, and alpine tundra. The diverse park/preserve habitats support an abundance of wildlife, such as Dall sheep, mountain goats, caribou, moose, bears, and wolves.

Wrangell–St. Elias was initially established by presidential proclamation as a national monument in 1978; was designated a World Heritage Site in 1979; and was legislatively established as a national park and preserve in 1980.

United States; **Mount Wrangell,** a still-active volcano, with vapor and gases issuing from fumaroles at its 14,163-foot summit; this volcano, located in the northwestern part of the park, last erupted in 1911; **Bagley Icefield,** the largest subpolar icefield in North America, stretching along 100 miles at the southern end of the park; **Malaspina Glacier,** larger than the state of Rhode Island it is North America's largest piedmont glacier, patterned with moraines and covering 100 square miles and located near the southeastern corner of the park; **Hubbard Glacier,** a massive, 80-mile-long tongue of ice that twists and turns from the north side of Canada's towering, 19,850-foot Mt. Logan, then enters the southeastern corner of the park and ends at Disenchantment Bay, where great chunks of its 300-foot-high face "calve" into the ocean; **Tyndall Glacier,** one of several glaciers at the head of Icy Bay in the southern end of the park, where glacial ice has dramatically retreated more than 20 miles during the past century; **Russell Glacier,** a 26-mile-long glacier between the Wrangell and St. Elias ranges; **Chitina River Valley,** an area largely covered with stands of white spruces, quaking aspens, and balsam poplars, and some areas of muskeg and black-spruce bogs, which provides the major access into the southern flanks of the Wrangells and from which numerous major Chitina tributaries descend from glaciers through steep, narrow gorges; **Chitistone Falls,** an impressive, 300-foot waterfall in the eastern Wrangells where the Chitistone River plunges down a sheer cliff into a narrow gorge and flows through 20-mile-long and up-to-4,000-foot-deep Chitistone Canyon; and **Kennicott Copper Mill,** a mine in the Chitina Valley unit of the national preserve that yielded 591,000 tons of copper and 900,000 ounces of silver between 1906 and 1938 and is listed on the National Register of Historic Places.

OUTSTANDING FEATURES

Among the many outstanding features of the park are the following: **Mount St. Elias,** at 18,008 feet, the second highest peak in the

PRACTICAL INFORMATION

When to Go

The park is open year-round. Summer is the most popular season, when cloudy and cool

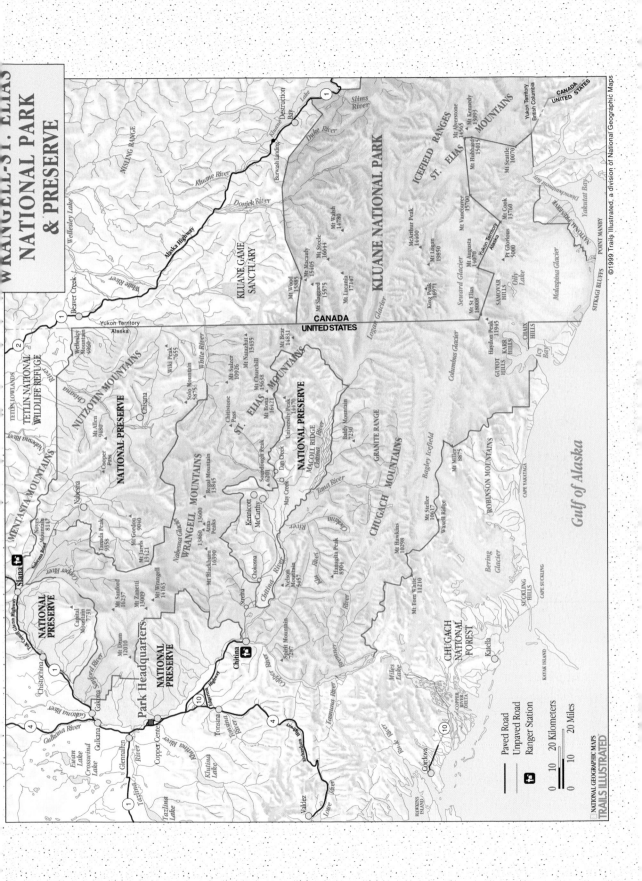

WRANGELL-ST. ELIAS NATIONAL PARK & PRESERVE

©1999 Trails Illustrated, a division of National Geographic Maps

CANADA
UNITED STATES

Yukon Territory
British Columbia

KLUANE NATIONAL PARK

ICEFIELD RANGES

ST. ELIAS MOUNTAINS

Mt Alverstone
14565

Mt Kennedy
13905

Mt Hubbard
15015

Mt Seattle
10070

Mt Vancouver
15700

Mt Cook
13760

Mt Augusta
14070

Mt St Elias
18008

Pt Glorious
5000

Yukon Territory
Alaska

SAMOVAR
HILLS

Oily
Lake

McArthur Peak
14400

Mt Logan
19850

Mt Macaulay
16644

Mt Walsh
14780

Mt Steele
16644

King Peak
16971

Seward Glacier

Mt Slaggard
15575

Mt Lucania
17147

Mt Wood
15885

Haydon Peak
11945

Malaspina Glacier

Logan Glacier

Columbus Glacier

GUYOT
HILLS

KARR
HILLS

CHAIX
HILLS

Icy
Bay

NATIONAL PARK
POINT MANBY

SITKAGI BLUFFS

Yakutat Bay

Disenchantment Bay

Kluane Lake

Destruction
Bay

Slims
River

Duke River

Burwash Landing

Kluane River

Donjek River

Alaska Highway

Wellesley Lake

White River

Beaver Creek

**KLUANE GAME
SANCTUARY**

CANADA
UNITED STATES

Yukon Territory
Alaska

Wellesley
Mountain
9069

Mt Bear
14831

Mt Natazhat
13435

Wiki Peak
7655

Mt Sulzer
10926

Mt Churchill
15638

Mt Bona
16421

University Peak
14470

ST. ELIAS MOUNTAINS

Solo Mountain
5850

Chitistone
Pass

Skolai Peak
6201

Dan Creek

NUTZOTIN MOUNTAINS

Chisana

Mt Allen
9480

Copper
Pass

NATIONAL PRESERVE

Regal Mountain
13845

WRANGELL MOUNTAINS

Nabesna Glacier

Nabesna

Tanada Peak
9358

Mt Gordon
9040

Mt Jarvis
13421

Noyes
Mountain
8147

Nabesna Road

MENTASTA MOUNTAINS

Slana

Copper River

Nabesna River

NATIONAL PRESERVE

Capital
Mountain
7731

Mt Sanford
16237

Mt Zanetti
13009

Mt Wrangell
14163

Mt Blackburn
16390

13860 13600
Atna
Peaks

Kennicott
McCarthy

Chokosna

May Creek

Nizina River

MACOLI RIDGE

Chitina River

NATIONAL PRESERVE

Baldy Mountain
8250

Tana River

GRANITE RANGE

CHUGACH MOUNTAINS

Bagley Icefield

ROBINSON MOUNTAINS

Mt Miller
8875

Bering
Glacier

Mt Stellar
10617

Mt Hawkins
10298

Mt Waxell Ridge

Mt Tom White
11210

Hanagita Peak
8904

Nelson
Mountain
7457

Chitina River
Strelna
Chitina

Copper River

Spirit Mountain
5287

Bremner River

Tana River

Tebay River

Miles
Lake

Bering River

STICKLING
HILLS

CAPE YAKATAGA

CAPE SUCKLING

KAYAK ISLAND

**CHUGACH
NATIONAL
FOREST**

Katalla

HAWKINS
ISLAND

COPPER RIVER
DELTA

Cordova

Tiekel River

Tsina River

Tazlina
Lake

Tsina River

Klutina
Lake

Tonsina River

Tonsina
Tonsina River

Richardson Highway

Edgerton Highway

Lowe River

Valdez

Copper River

Chitistone River

Park Headquarters

NATIONAL PRESERVE

Mt Drum
12010

Copper Center

Glennallen

Gakona
Gulkana
Gakona River

Tazlina
River

Klutina River

Tolsona
Lake

Chistochina

Chisana River

Mt Sanford

Tok Cutoff (Glenn Highway)

Ewan
Lake

Crosswind
Lake

Gulkana River

Gakona Junction

Gulf of Alaska

Legend

Paved Road
Unpaved Road
Ranger Station

0 10 20 Kilometers
0 10 20 Miles

NATIONAL GEOGRAPHIC MAPS
TRAILS ILLUSTRATED

▲ *Boreal forest and beaver pond in Wrangell-St. Elias National Park and Preserve, Alaska*

weather is prevalent, although clear, hot days are not uncommon in July. Wildflowers are abundant in June. August and September tend to be cool and wet, but with fewer mosquitoes than July. Autumn can be beautiful, with foliage colors and a dusting of new snow on the mountain peaks, but this season is short. Winters are cold and dark, with temperatures dropping to -50 degrees. Though the average snow cover is two feet, days are often clear. In the spring, clear skies, increasingly longer days, and warming temperatures break winter's hold on the land with dramatic speed. Spring is an excellent time for crosscountry skiing.

How to Get There

By Car: From Anchorage, take the Glenn Highway (State Route 1) to Glennallen. South from Glennallen, the Richardson Highway (State Route 4) runs about ten miles to the park/preserve headquarters. From there, the highway continues south, to the Edgerton Highway (State Route 10), which leads southeast to Chitina. From there, the rough, unpaved, 62-mile Chitina-McCarthy Road, with three unbridged river crossings, leads into the Chitina Valley area of the park and preserve. Northeast from Glennallen, the Tok Cutoff Glenn Highway (State Route 1) runs along the northwestern boundary of the park/preserve; from which the unpaved, 46-mile Nabesna Road branches at Slana and enters the northern unit of the national preserve. Visitors are urged to check on current road conditions since these two access routes are not regularly maintained.

By Air: McCarthy has a maintained airstrip and is served by regular mail flights. Charter flights are available in most communities, including Anchorage, Fairbanks, Northway, Glennallen, Cordova, Valdez, Tok, and Yakutat. Cordova and Yakutat are served daily by commercial jets.

By Train: The Alaska Railroad (800-544-0552) offers service from Anchorage to Whittier, which is linked to Valdez via the Alaska Marine Highway.

By Bus: In summer, buses run regularly from Anchorage to Valdez, with stops in Glennallen.

By Ferry: The Alaska Marine Highway (800-642-0066) serves Valdez.

Fees and Permits

There are no entrance fees. Fishing requires a state license, which is available in gateway communities. Backcountry permits are not required, but travelers are strongly encouraged to complete a backcountry itinerary form, available at any park office.

Visitor Information

Visitor information is available at park headquarters, just south of Glennallen on the Richardson Highway, or at the district ranger stations in Slana, Chitina, and Yakutat.

Facilities

There are no National Park Service facilities wthinin the park/preserve. Glennallen has a supermarket, and supplies are available in McCarthy.

Handicapped Accessibility

The park is all wilderness landscape. There are no specific facilities for the handicapped.

Medical Services

First aid is not available in the park, but there is a clinic in Glennallen, about ten miles north of park headquarters.

Safety and Regulations

For your safety and enjoyment and for the protection of the park, please follow these regulations and suggestions:

- Backcountry hikers must be self-sufficient, carry enough food to cover unexpected delays, and be prepared for the wilderness. Assistance may be days or miles away, so visitors are cautioned to be extraordinarily careful when trekking into this vast moun-

tainous region. Appropriate survival gear and skills are essential.

- Lakes and streams may be difficult, if not impossible, to cross. River crossings pose one of the greatest hazards in the Wrangells.

- The National Park Service urges visitors to please respect private property and subsistence equipment, such as fishnets and traps, and not to trespass on private lands.

- Hunting, fishing, and trapping are permitted only in the preserve with an Alaska license.

- Access to national parklands can be difficult because of the private land surrounding the park. Careful planning is advised before adventuring in this vast area.

ACTIVITIES

Options include hiking, horseback riding, pack trips, float trips, kayaking, lake fishing, mountaineering, and cross-country skiing. Most visitors to the community of McCarthy explore the historic Kennicott Copper Mine. Further information is available in the park's newspaper, *K'elt'aeni* (the Ahtna Athabaskan word for Mount Wrangell, roughly meaning "the One that controls the weather").

Mountaineering

St. Elias Alpine Guides provide guided mountaineering expertise. Guided hiking trips of various lengths are also offered. (907-345-9048)

Hiking Trails

Among the available trails are: **Nugget Creek Trail,** a fairly strenuous, 16-mile, 1,000-foot climb beginning at the end of the 2.5-mile Nugget Creek–Kotsina Road (which branches from the Chitina-McCarthy Road at Mile 13.5) and reaches a public-use cabin below 16,390-foot Mt. Blackburn in the Wrangell Mountains; and **Dixie Pass Trail,** a strenuous, ten-mile, 3,600-foot climb into the Wrangells, branching about a mile from the start of the Nugget Creek Trail.

◀ *Mount St. Elias in Wrangell–St. Elias National Park and Preserve, Alaska*

OUTSTANDING FEATURES

Lodging and Dining

Rustic accommodations are provided at privately operated fishing camps, guide cabins, and lodges in various parts of the park. Kennicott Glacier Lodge in McCarthy provides accommodations near the historic Kennicott Mine. Motels and restaurants provide standard tourist-travel services in major communities along the highways near the park and in the coastal communities of Yakutat, Valdez, and Cordova. Visitors are urged to make reservations well in advance.

Campgrounds and Cabins

Scattered remote cabins throughout the region accommodate backcountry parties, and the Bureau of Land Management and the state of Alaska run campgrounds along the Richardson Highway, Tok Cutoff, and Edgerton Highway.

Backcountry Camping

Tent camping is permitted anywhere within the park, except on private property. Permits are not required, but travelers are encouraged to complete an itinerary at any park office. Visitors must be prepared to be completely self-sufficient and thoroughly prepared for weather and other remote-wilderness challenges.

FLORA AND FAUNA (Partial Listings)

Mammals: Alaskan brown (grizzly) and black bears, Dall sheep, mountain goat, barren ground caribou, moose, lynx, gray wolf, coyote, red fox, wolverine, pine marten, mink, river otter, least and shorttail weasels, hoary marmot, beaver, muskrat, snowshoe hare, arctic ground squirrel, red squirrel, harbor seal, Steller sea lion, harbor and Dall porpoises, and killer (orca) whales.

Birds: red-throated and common loons, red-necked grebe, double-crested and pelagic cormorants, trumpeter and tundra swans, green-winged and blue-winged teals, mallard, pintail, shoveler, wigeon, greater scaup, harlequin duck, oldsquaw, surf and white-winged scoters, common and Barrow's goldeneyes, bufflehead, common and red-breasted mergansers, osprey, bald and golden eagles, red-tailed hawk, northern harrier, sharp-shinned hawk, goshawk, merlin, gyrfalcon, spruce and ruffed grouse, ptarmigans (willow, rock, and white-tailed), black oystercatcher, greater and lesser yellowlegs, sandpipers (solitary, spotted, and upland), surfbird, common snipe, red-necked phalarope, gulls (Bonaparte's, mew, herring, and glaucous-winged), black-legged kittiwake, arctic tern, common murre, pigeon guillemot, marbled and ancient murrelets, owls (western screech, great horned, snowy, boreal, great gray, short-eared, and northern saw-whet), northern hawk-owl, rufous hummingbird, belted kingfisher, woodpeckers (downy, hairy, three-toed, and black-backed), flicker, olive-sided and alder flycatchers, western wood pewee, Say's phoebe, horned lark, swallows (tree, violet-green, bank, and cliff), gray and Steller's jays, black-billed magpie, northwestern crow, raven, chickadees (black-capped, boreal, and chestnut-backed), red-breasted nuthatch, brown creeper, winter wren, dipper, golden-crowned and ruby-crowned kinglets, Townsend's solitaire, thrushes (gray-cheeked, Swainson's, hermit, and varied), robin, northern wheatear, Bohemian waxwing, warblers (orange-crowned, yellow, Townsend's, yellow-rumped or myrtle, blackpoll, and Wilson's), northern waterthrush, sparrows (tree, chipping, savannah, fox, song, Lincoln's, golden-crowned, and white-crowned), dark-eyed junco, lapland and Smith's longspurs, snow bunting, red-winged blackbird, rosy finch, pine grosbeak, red and white-winged crossbills, common redpoll, and pine siskin.

Trees, Shrubs, and Flowers: spruces (Sitka, white, and black), western and mountain hemlocks, tamarack, balsam poplar, quaking aspen, paper and dwarf birches, willows, alders, salmonberry, devil's club, Labrador tea, blueberry, bearberry, mountain heather, glaucous gentian, mountain avens, and lupine.

NEARBY POINTS OF INTEREST

The surrounding area offers other exciting natural and historical attractions. Canada's Kluane National Park and Kluane Game Sanctuary adjoin the park to the east. Tetlin National Wildlife Refuge borders the park to the north. The U.S. Bureau of Land Management's Gulkana River area is just northwest of Glennallen. Tongass and Chugach national forests border the park to the south. Denali National Park and Preserve are to the northwest. Glacier Bay National Park and Preserve and Klondike Gold Rush and Sitka national historical parks are to the southeast. Kenai Fjords National Park and Katmai National Park and Preserve are to the southwest.

OTHER NATIONAL PARK UNITS IN THE ALASKA REGION

▲ Totem pole amidst the forest in Sitka National Historical Park, Alaska

Other National Park Units in the Alaska Region

Alagnak Wild River

**c/o Katmai National Park and
Preserve
P.O. Box 7
King Salmon, AK 99613-0007
907-246-3305**

This 30,800-acre unit in southwest Alaska protects this remote wilderness river that heads up in two lakes in adjacent Katmai National Preserve, flows westward through a scenic canyon containing dangerous rapids, and winds through open, gently rolling country and wetlands. West of the river, the Alagnak flows into Kvichak Bay. Nearly 70 miles of the river are used for whitewater float trips, for which backcountry permits are required. The area supports an abundance of wildlife, and its waters are inhabited by rainbow trout, Arctic grayling, and five species of salmon. While there are no visitor facilities, several commercial fishing lodges are located on adjacent private lands, and lodging and meals are provided in King Salmon. Access is by way of scheduled flights to King Salmon and chartered flights from there to Kukaklek Lake in Katmai National Preserve.

Aniakchak National Monument and Preserve

**c/o Katmai National Park and
Preserve
P.O. Box 7
King Salmon, AK 99613-0007
907-246-3305**

This 137,176-acre national monument and the adjacent 465,603-acre national preserve on the Alaska Peninsula in southwest Alaska protect the remains of an ancient, six-mile-wide, 3,500-foot-deep volcanic caldera, along with the Aniakchak Wild River and the rocky shores of Aniakchak and Amber bays along the Pacific Ocean. The caldera, one of the largest in the world, was formed by a colossal erup-

tion that undermined or blew out the inner part of a 7,000-foot volcano, the summit of which then collapsed. From blue-green, spring-fed Surprise Lake that occupies a corner of the caldera, the swiftly flowing Aniakchak River rushes through a 2,000-foot-deep canyon in the crater's rim known as "the Gates" and descends southeastward for 27 miles to Aniakchak Bay. The monument and preserve include diverse habitats along Bristol Bay's coastal plain and wild bays, inlets, and offshore islands, supporting an abundance of such wildlife as seabirds, migratory waterfowl, and marine mammals.

No visitor facilities are provided. Access to the monument and preserve is by way of scheduled flights to King Salmon. Charter flights are also available from King Salmon to Surprise Lake, though inclement weather often prevents access. The National Park Service advises visitors to leave their itinerary with a ranger at monument headquarters.

Bering Land Bridge National Preserve

**P.O. Box 220
Nome, AK 99762-0220
907-443-2522**

This national preserve on the Seward Peninsula in northwest Alaska protects a remnant of the former land bridge between North America and Asia. This natural stretch of land, now about 100 feet beneath sea level, is believed to have been the route by which humans and many species of plants and animals reached North America more than 10,000 years ago, when the ocean level was lower. The national preserve is located only 60 miles across the Bering Sea from the Siberian mainland of Russia. The 2,698,000-acre area contains numerous significant paleontological and archaeological sites and vast expanses of coastal flats, wetlands, lakes, streams, hot springs, lagoons, sea cliffs, and coastal waters. These diverse habitats support an abundance of wildlife, including seabirds, migratory waterfowl, grizzly and polar bears, moose, gray wolf, wolverine, red and arctic foxes, the reintroduced musk-oxen, walrus, seals, and whales. Native Alaskans continue to use the area, as they have for thousands of years, for their subsistence hunting, fishing, and gathering needs.

The preserve provides no visitor facilities. Primitive camping is permitted, but visitors are urged to respect private lands, structures, and subsistence facilities within the preserve. Information on the preserve, travel precautions, guide services, flight access, and lodging and meals in Nome and Kotzebue are available by contacting the preserve headquarters.

Cape Krusenstern National Monument

P.O. Box 1029
Kotzebue, AK 99752-1029
907-442-3890

This 650,000-acre national monument north of the Arctic Circle in northwest Alaska contains a wealth of archaeological information about the Native Alaskan culture, presenting an unbroken record of these people's prehistory, dating back to approximately 2300 B.C. The monument protects 66 miles of coastline along the Chukchi Sea and Kotzebue Sound, as well as an unusual ridged shore of a series of 114 ocean beach ridges spanning a period of roughly 8,000 to 10,000 years. These ridges, forming a four-mile-long arc around Cape Krusenstern and rising to about seven feet in height, were created by wind-driven ice, wave-driven gravel, ocean currents, and tides. A large freshwater lagoon lies behind the ridges.

Among the monument's highlights are spectacular scenic landscapes, wildflowers, challenging hiking opportunities along the coast of Chukchi Sea, and an abundance of wildlife, including the bearded seal, other marine mammals, and migratory waterfowl. The monument provides no visitor facilities. Access is by way of scheduled flights from Anchorage and Fairbanks to Kotzebue and by charter flights or rental boats from there to the monument.

Iditarod National Historic Trail

U.S. Bureau of Land Management
6881 Abbott Loop Road
Anchorage, AK 99507
907-267-1246

This network of late 19th century and early 20th century Alaska gold rush trails extends 2,400 miles between Seward and Nome. The annual 1,100-mile Iditarod Sled Dog Race is run along the trail from Anchorage to Nome. Stretches of the trail are also popular for mountain biking, ski races, snowshoeing, and the world's longest snow-machine race.

Klondike Gold Rush National Historical Park

P.O. Box 517
Skagway, AK 99840-0517
907-983-2921
or
117 S. Main St.
Seattle, WA 98104
206-553-7220

This national historical park commemorates one of the most spectacular gold rushes in North America. In the summer of 1896, gold was discovered in a tributary of the Klondike River in Canada's Yukon Territory. News of the shipment of gold aboard a boat from Skagway to Seattle triggered a stampede of between 20,000 and 30,000 fortune hunters who poured into hastily built tent and shack towns in Skagway and Dyea in 1898.

This 13,191-acre, four-unit park in and near Skagway in southeast Alaska and in the Pioneer Square Historic District of Seattle, Washington, features restored buildings in the historic district of downtown Skagway, including the old White Pass and Yukon Railroad Depot housing the park's visitor center at Broadway and 2nd Avenue and the Mascot Saloon at Broadway and 3rd. The park also includes the Dyea town site and the U.S. stretches of the Chilkoot and White Pass trails. In the summer, the Chilkoot Trail is a popular three- to five-day hike that crosses into Canada. Experienced and well-outfitted hikers climb this challenging route that begins in lush coastal rainforest, follows the Taiya River Canyon, and climbs steeply to Chilkoot Pass on the U.S.–Canada border. The visitor centers, in Skagway and at 117 S. Main Street., Seattle, provide interpretive exhibits, programs, and publications. Access to Skagway by car is from Whitehorse and Carcross on Route 2 in Canada to White Pass and down to Skagway. Other options are scheduled flights to Skagway and by boat, including the Alaska state ferry system.

Kobuk Valley National Park

**P.O. Box 1029
Kotzebue, AK 99752-1029
907-442-3890**

This 1,750,736-acre national park, north of
the Arctic Circle in northwest Alaska, protects
a vast and magnificent wilderness encompassing a broad, largely enclosed, mountain basin
straddling the northernmost reaches of boreal
forest and the treeless arctic tundra, as well as
the meandering Kobuk River and the spectacular, 16,000-acre expanse of the Great Kobuk
Sand Dunes that rise to about 150 feet—the
largest area of active sand dunes in the arctic
region of North America. A tributary of the
Kobuk, the Salmon River, has also been designated a national wild and scenic river.

Archaeological sites, such as Onion
Portage, are revealing more than 12,000 years
of human occupation in this region of Alaska,
and Native Alaskan subsistence hunting and
fishing are among the authorized uses of this
park. In late winter and spring, the native people hunt a variety of wildlife for meat, skins, and
oil, as they have for thousands of years. In summer, they net fish and gather plants for food
and herbal medicines; in late summer, they har-
vest wild berries. In autumn, they hunt caribou
as the animals migrate southward to spend winter in the southern part of the park and adjacent
Selawik National Wildlife Refuge. Visitors are
urged to be respectful of the native people and
not interfere with their subsistence camps, fishnets, and other facilities; public hunting is not
permitted in the park.

The park's ecologically diverse habitats
support a tremendous variety of wildlife.
Kobuk Valley is the autumn and winter range
for part of the western arctic herd of barren
ground caribou, which numbers more than
300,000 animals. Other mammals include
moose, Dall sheep, grizzly and black bears,
gray wolf, arctic and red foxes, wolverine,
pine marten, mink, weasel, porcupine, beaver,
muskrat, snowshoe hare, and lemming.
Visitors are cautioned to be especially on the
lookout for the grizzlies, give them lots of distance, and avoid making them feel threatened.

The many species of birds include loons,
sandhill cranes, tundra swans, Canada and
emperor geese, numerous ducks (including
green-winged teal, shoveler, pintail, oldsquaw,
and red-breasted merganser), golden eagle,
gyrfalcon, peregrine falcon, spruce grouse,
willow and rock ptarmigan, snowy and great
gray owls, belted kingfisher, gray jay, raven,
boreal and black-capped chickadees, Siberian
tit or gray-headed chickadee (an Asian
species), thrushes (varied, hermit, Swainson's,
and gray-cheeked), bluethroats (an Asian
species), dipper, Bohemian waxwing, warblers
(orange-crowned, yellow, yellow-rumped or
myrtle, blackpoll, and Wilson's), northern
waterthrush, snow bunting, white-winged
crossbill, and pine grosbeak.

Among the flora are white and black
spruces, paper and dwarf birches, alder, balsam poplar, quaking aspen, willows, common
juniper, Labrador tea, red currant, lowbush
cranberry, salmonberry, blueberry, crowberry,
fireweed, wild rose, western columbine, shootingstar, twinflower, larkspurs, arctic paintbrush,
and fairy lady's-slipper.

One of the pleasures of visiting this park is a
float trip by raft, canoe, kayak, or motorboat on
the placid Kobuk River. One of the side treks
from the river is the easy hike to the Great Kobuk
Sand Dunes, but visitors are cautioned to beware
of quicksand when walking near Kavet Creek.
Even though backcountry permits are not currently required, it is wise for visitors to leave a
copy of their itinerary at the information center
in Kotzebue. The National Park Service also provides travel information and precautions, including advice on hiking and camping in bear country and when to expect hoards of biting insects
and mosquitoes (the latter are generally at their
worst from mid-June through mid-July). The park
provides no overnight accommodations or campgrounds. Lodgings are offered in Kotzebue and
in the villages of Ambler upriver from the park
and Kiana downriver from the park. Access is by
scheduled flights from Anchorage or Fairbanks
to Kotzebue and by flights from there to Ambler,
Kiana, and elsewhere.

Lake Clark National Park and Preserve

**4230 University Drive, Suite 311
Anchorage, AK 99508-4626
907-781-2218**

This national park and preserve, partly bordering Cook Inlet in southwest Alaska, protects a

scenic wilderness of awesomely rugged mountains, including the glacier-draped Chigmit Mountains, which overlap the southern end of the Alaska Range and the northern end of the Aleutian Range. Two still-active, steaming volcanoes—10,197-foot Redoubt and 10,016-foot Iliamna—are the highest points in the park.

Also within this incredible 2,619,858-acre national park and adjacent 1,410,641-acre national preserve are many wild rivers, plunging waterfalls, coastal fjords, temperate rainforest, boreal forest, wetlands, and lakes. The largest of the latter is 48-mile-long Lake Clark, a popular resting and feeding area for great numbers of waterfowl. The park and preserve consist of diverse ecosystems representative of many parts of Alaska. Along the eastern flanks of the mountains are dense spruce forests, and along Cook Inlet are rugged coastal cliffs inhabited by rookeries of seabirds. On the western flanks of the mountain are tundra-covered foothills that descend to stands of boreal forest. Three rivers—the Tlikakila, which is entirely within the park and flows into Lake Clark, and the Chilikadrotna and Mulchatna in both the park and preserve—have been designated national wild and scenic rivers.

Among the mammals are Alaskan brown and black bears, caribou, Dall sheep, moose, lynx, gray wolf, red fox, pine marten, mink, river otter, least and shorttail weasels, muskrats, and ground squirrels. Birds include loons (red-throated, Pacific, and common), tundra and trumpeter swans, green-winged teal, harlequin duck, oldsquaw, scoters, common and Barrow's goldeneyes, common and red-breasted mergansers, osprey, goshawk, sharp-shinned hawk, bald and golden eagles, peregrine falcon, gyrfalcon, spruce grouse, ptarmigans (rock, willow, and white-tailed), common snipe, glaucous-winged gull, black-legged kittiwake, arctic tern, common murre, pigeon guillemot, marbled and ancient murrelets, tufted and horned puffins, owls (great horned, snowy, boreal, and great gray), northern hawk-owl, belted kingfisher, woodpeckers (downy, hairy, three-toed, and black-backed), olive-sided and alder flycatchers, swallows (tree, violet-green, bank, and cliff), gray jay, black-billed magpie, raven, black-capped and boreal chickadees, red-breasted nuthatch, brown creeper, dipper, golden-crowned and ruby-crowned kinglets, thrushes (gray-cheeked, Swainson's, hermit, and varied), robin, Bohemian waxwing, warblers (orange-crowned, yellow, yellow-rumped or myrtle, blackpoll, and Wilson's), northern waterthrush, sparrows (tree, savannah, fox, song, Lincoln's, golden-crowned, and white-crowned), dark-eyed junco, rosy finch, pine grosbeak, white-winged crossbill, and redpoll.

Among the trees are spruces (white, black, and Sitka), paper and dwarf birches, balsam poplar, and quaking aspen. Shrubs include shrubby cinquefoil, Labrador tea, bog rosemary, alpine bearberry, wild rose, three species of blueberry, crowberry, lingonberry, high- and low-bush cranberry, red currant, cloudberry, and salmonberry. Of the numerous wildflowers are fireweed, forget-me-not, iris, mountain avens, king's-crown, gentian, mountain saxifrage, rock jasmine, bunchberry, and moss campion.

The National Park Service cautions visitors to beware of bears and moose and urges hikers to keep a safe distance and avoid threatening or startling these animals, as their behavior is unpredictable. The park headquarters offers important information on traveling and camping in bear country, travel information and precautions, and regulations. There are no roads or established campgrounds within the park. Two lodges are available: Alaska's Wilderness Lodge (open June through September) at Port Alsworth on the southern shore of Lake Clark in the preserve; and Silver Salmon Creek Lodge (open mid-May through September) in the park. Access is by charter float planes from Anchorage. Other flights are offered from Kenai, Homer, and Iliamna.

Noatak National Preserve

P.O. Box 1029
Kotzbue, AK 99752-1029
907-442-3760

This 6,570,000-acre national preserve, encompassing the vast, mountain-bordered Noatak River Basin north of the Arctic Circle in northwest Alaska, protects an expansive tundra wilderness that supports an abundance of wildlife. The Noatak, a national wild and scenic river, is the largest complete river system still in its natural condition in the United States.

The scenic highlight of the preserve is the ruggedly magnificent, 65-mile-long Grand Canyon of the Noatak. So outstanding are the natural and unsullied qualities of the national preserve that the United Nations has designated it a "Man in the Biosphere Reserve." The name "Noatak" comes from the old Inupiat word Noataq meaning "passage to the interior," and indeed the river's headwaters are high in the Gates of the Arctic National Park, and it flows for 250 miles across the tundra of the national preserve. No river surpasses the Noatak as a wilderness recreation river; rafting, canoeing, and kayaking are popular.

The Noatak Basin is also a major migration route to and from summer calving grounds on the Arctic Coastal Plain for the western arctic barren ground caribou herd that numbers more than 300,000 animals. Other mammals include grizzly and black bears, moose, Dall sheep, lynx, gray wolf, coyote, red and arctic foxes, wolverine, pine marten, mink, river otter, least and shorttail weasels, snowshoe hare, arctic ground squirrel, and lemming. Among the birds are loons, sandhill crane, tundra swan, Canada goose, wigeon, pintail, shoveler, oldsquaw, red-breasted merganser, golden plover, common snipe, red-necked phalarope, golden eagle, gyrfalcon, rock ptarmigan, raven, lapland longspur, and snow bunting.

Native Alaskan subsistence hunting, fishing, and gathering are permitted to continue in the preserve—a tradition dating back thousands of years. Public hunting is also allowed under state regulations during the designated season. Travel information, precautions, regulations, and important advice on traveling and camping in bear country are available from the national preserve headquarters. Access is by way of scheduled flights from Anchorage or Fairbanks to Kotzebue and by other flights from there to the preserve for backpacking and fishing excursions.

Sitka National Historical Park

P.O. Box 738
Sitka, AK 99835-0738
907-747-6281

This park, in and adjacent to the city of Sitka on Baranof Island in southeast Alaska, protects and interprets the sites of the Tlingit Indians' Kiksadi fort and the Battle of Sitka, where these native people were defeated by Russian colonists and their Aleut Indian allies in 1804. In 1799, the Russian-American Company, managed by Aleksandr Baranov, established a Russian fur-trading post just north of today's Sitka, profiting from the exploitation of sea otters and fur seals that inhabited Alaskan coastal waters in abundance. In 1802, the Tlingit Indians attacked and destroyed the fledgling colony in a desperate attempt to end Russia's claim to the Indians' traditional lands. But two years later, a fleet of four ships returned, loaded with an army of 1,000 Russians and their Aleut Indian allies. The Battle of Sitka ended with the defeat of 700 Tlingits, allowing the Russians to re-establish their colony. By the mid-19th century, however, the population of the fur-bearing marine mammals and the local Russian economy had dramatically declined, and in 1867, Russia sold Alaska to the United States for $7.2 million.

This main unit of the 106-acre, two-unit national historical park contains a visitor center with interpretive exhibits and programs on Tlingit history and cultural traditions. It also houses the Southeast Alaska Indian Cultural Center, where Indian students are taught traditional artistic skills and techniques in weaving, basketry, silver working, and wood and stone carving and where visitors may observe native artists at work. A loop trail from the visitor center leads through a lush, temperate rainforest of large Sitka spruces and western hemlocks; then passes numerous, boldly carved Tlingit and Haida totems; and reaches the battle and fort sites at the end of the point where Indian River flows into Sitka Sound. Another trail crosses the river and leads to two picnic areas and the Russian Memorial. The entrance to this unit of the park is about a half-mile from Sitka's business district and can be reached on foot by following Lincoln Street. Buses and taxis are also available.

Adjacent to the park is the state of Alaska's Sheldon Jackson Museum, providing outstanding interpretive exhibits of the Native American cultures of Alaska and containing one of the best collections anywhere of Alaskan cultural materials. For further information, call 907-747-8981.

The park also features the Russian Bishop's House at Lincoln and Monastery streets in downtown Sitka, which was the Russian Orthodox Church's official residence for the Bishop of Sitka. This restored log structure, dating from the 1840s, is one of the very few remaining examples of Russian colonial architecture in North America. Inside are the Bishop's personal quarters, the Chapel of Annunciation, and several rooms presenting historical exhibits. Nearby on Lincoln Street, but not within the park, is St. Michael's Cathedral, a replica of the original onion-steepled church dating from 1848, which was destroyed by fire in 1966.

Lodging and meals are available in Sitka. Access to the city is by way of scheduled flights from Seattle and from elsewhere in Alaska or by boat, including the Alaska State ferry system and cruise ships.

Yukon-Charley Rivers National Preserve

P.O. Box 167
Eagle, AK 99738-0167
907-547-2233

This 2,526,509-acre national preserve in east-central Alaska protects 115 miles of the mighty, 1,800-mile-long Yukon River—the world's fourth largest river—and all 106 miles of its major tributary, the beautiful Charley River, which has been designated a national wild and scenic river. The preserve also encompasses the remote 1.1-million-acre wilderness watershed of the Charley. Many consider the Charley to be Alaska's most magnificent river as it dashes from upland tundra; flows through valley boreal forests of white spruces, paper birches, and quaking aspens; passes beneath sheer bluffs; and meanders across expanses of boggy muskeg with stands of black spruces and tamaracks. The preserve's outstanding ecological diversity is due in part to the fact that most of the Yukon-Charley area remained unglaciated when most of Alaska was buried beneath continental glacial ice more than 20,000 years ago.

Mammals of the preserve include barren ground caribou, Dall sheep, moose, grizzly and black bears, lynx, wolverine, pine marten, mink, least and shorttail weasels, river otter, gray wolf, coyote, red fox, porcupine, beaver, muskrat, snowshoe hare, arctic ground squirrel, red squirrel, and northern bog and brown lemmings.

Among the birds are Pacific and common loons, trumpeter swan, greater white-fronted and Canada geese, sandhill crane, green- and blue-winged teals, mallard, pintail, shoveler, American wigeon, canvasback, oldsquaw, common goldeneye, bufflehead, red-breasted merganser, osprey, bald and golden eagles, peregrine falcon, owls (great horned, snowy, boreal, and great gray), northern hawk-owl, spruce grouse, willow and rock ptarmigan, ruffed and sharp-tailed grouse, sandhill crane, golden plover, common snipe, belted kingfisher, woodpeckers (downy, hairy, three-toed, and black-backed), olive-sided and alder flycatchers, Say's phoebe, gray jay, raven, black-capped and boreal chickadees, dipper, ruby-crowned kinglet, mountain bluebird, Townsend's solitaire, thrushes (gray-cheeked, Swainson's, hermit, and varied), robin, American pipit, Bohemian waxwing, warblers (orange-crowned, yellow, yellow-rumped or myrtle, blackpoll, and Wilson's), northern waterthrush, sparrows (tree, savannah, fox, and white-crowned), rosy finch, pine grosbeak, white-winged crossbill, and redpoll.

Canoeing, kayaking, rafting, primitive camping, and fishing are popular activities in the preserve. Public hunting is also permitted during the designated season. Visitors are urged to respect private properties, fishing camps, and cabins and not to disturb subsistence facilities, such as fishnets and fish drying racks. No access roads, established trails, or campgrounds are provided. Outfitting and guide services are available, and the National Park Service offers important information on traveling and camping in bear country and other safety precautions.

The headquarters and a Bureau of Land Management campground are located in Eagle on the Yukon River, upriver from and 12 miles south of the preserve. This town is reached from Tetlin Junction on the Alaska Highway, north 161 miles on the gravel Taylor Highway, which is usually open from mid-April to mid-October. The Steese Highway, open year-round, runs 162 miles from Fairbanks to Circle, downriver from and 14 miles north of the preserve. Lodging and meals are offered in Eagle, Circle, and Central and at Circle Hot Springs Resort. Scheduled airline flights serve Fairbanks; scheduled air taxis serve Eagle and

85

Circle year-round as weather permits; and chartered flights take visitors to a number of landing strips in and near the preserve.

Friends of the Parks Organizations

Denali Citizens Council
P.O. Box 78
Denali Park, AK 99755
907-683-2597 (May-September)

Denali Foundation
P.O. Box 212
Denali Park, AK 99755
907-683-2597 (May-September)

Friends of Glacier Bay
P.O. Box 135
Gustavus, AK 99826
907-697-2287

Friends of Katmai
P.O. Box 573
King Salmon, AK 99613

Friends of Kenai Fjords
P.O. Box 267
Seward, AK 99664
907-224-3175

Friends of Kennicott
(Wrangell-St. Elias National Park and Preserve)
3018 Alder Circle
Anchorage, AK 99508
907-243-8398

Iditarod National Historic Trail, Inc.
P.O. Box 2323
Seward, AK 99664

Iditarod Trail Committee
P.O. Box 870800
Wasilla, AK 99687
907-376-5155

Sitka Conservation Society
P.O. Box 316
Sitka, AK 99835
907-747-7509

Wrangell Mountains Center
P.O. Box MXY
Glen Allen, AK 99588
907-554-4464

Cooperating Associations

Alaska Geographic Society, The
P.O. Box 93370
Anchorage, AK 99509
907-258-2515

Alaska Natural History Association
401 West 1st Avenue
Anchorage, AK 99501
907-274-8440

Alaska Public Lands Information Center
605 West 4th Avenue, Suite 105
Anchorage, AK 99501
907-271-2737

National Trust for Historic Preservation
1785 Massachusetts Avenue, N.W.
Washington, D.C. 20036
202-673-4000

Student Conservation Association
1800 N. Kent Street
Arlington, VA 22209
703-524-2441

◀ *Alsek Lake in Glacier Bay National Park and Preserve, Alaska*

LOCAL COLOR

The Wildlife

"Texas" means friend.

Texas was a country before it was a state.

25 languages.

65 nationalities.

Texans believe life is too important to be dull.

The Wildflowers

The state flower is the Bluebonnet.

Over 5,000 species of wildflowers.

There's even a Wildflower Center (Thanks to Lady Bird Johnson).

Texas does not have blue grass. It just seems that way.

It's like a whole other country.®

Even the vacations are bigger in Texas. From the yarn-spinning charm of our native citizenry to hills carpeted with our native flowers, you'll find it all in Texas. It's more than you think. It's like a whole other country. For your free Texas travel guide, you can visit our web site at 💻 **www.TravelTex.com** or call us at ☎ **1-800-8888-TEX (Ext. 1290).** So give us a call, y'all.

NPCA Checks
Save Our Parks!

Every order helps preserve our country's most precious areas. Every time you order, royalties go directly to the National Parks and Conservation Association.

Return Address Labels - six scenes match your checks!

Hemp Checkbook Cover features the NPCA logo

Cotton Covers- select your favorite scene

Acadia

Everglades

Yellowstone

Arches

Smoky Mountains

Yosemite

utiful rotating
es features
Great Smoky
ntains, Yosemite,
es, Yellowstone,
ia, and Everglades
nal Parks.

N A T I O N A L P A R K S C H E C K S O R D E R F O R M

k Your Choice Below:	200 Singles	150 Duplicates	Total
ational Parks Check Series (6 designs) (NP)	❏ $15.95	❏ $17.95	$_____
40 National Parks Labels (6 designs) (NP-LB) ....Add $12.95			$_____
kbook Covers:			
emp Logo Cover (HNP-UQLO)...Add $14.95			$_____
otton Cover (CNP -UQLO)..Add $11.95			$_____

elect Scene: ❏ Acadia ❏ Everglades ❏ Yellowstone
❏ Arches ❏ Smoky Mountains ❏ Yosemite

SUBTOTAL	$_____	
Add 6.5% tax *for Minnesota residents only*	$_____	
Delivery ❏ $1.95 per item *OR* PRIORITY ❏ $3.95 per item	$_____	
TOTAL ENCLOSED:	$_____	
	GD	

IMPORTANT! Include the following with this form:

❏ Voided check indicating a starting number # _____ for your new order
  (If none given we will start your order at 101)
❏ Deposit ticket from the same account
❏ Three lines of personalization for matching labels: *(see left side!)*

_____
_____
_____

❏ Daytime Telephone Number:(_____)_____
  (CONFIDENTIAL - in case of questions about your order only)

Please allow 3-5 weeks processing & delivery OR 1-3 weeks for PRIORITY delivery

To order, send complete form to:
Message!Products   *or fax to:*
P.O. Box 64800   1-800-790-6684
St. Paul, MN   *or order online!*
55164-0800   **www.messagecheck.com**

QUESTIONS? 1-800-243-2565

ment type
Check enclosed–make payable to: Message!Products™ *No COD's*
Debit my checking account (CHECK ORDERS ONLY) Signature_____
Charge to: ❏ Visa ❏ Mastercard ❏ American Express ❏ Discover
No._____ Exp. Date___/___ Signature_____

IF WE DON'T PROTECT THEM, WHO WILL?

LEND YOUR VOICE TO HELP SAVE OUR CROWN JEWELS.

The national parks belong to you and me, and they are the most important, meaningful and irreplaceable resource we have to give to future generations.

Unfortunately, our parks are in crisis! Almost every single one of the 378 national park units is troubled by problems of overcrowding, pollution and destructive uses that threaten to permanently damage these precious places...but there is hope.

For 80 years the National Parks and Conservation Association has been the only private, non-profit citizens' organization dedicated solely to preserving and protecting our National Park System. Over the years, some of our accomplishments have included: saving parks from toxic mining plans and nearby nuclear waste dumps, brokering pollution-abating air quality agreements, and working with Congress to implement concessions reform — that stopped businesses from profiting unfairly from the parks!

Our work is far from over and we need your help now! Please join National Parks and Conservation Association and lend your voice to the nearly 400,000 others who help us in our daily fight to save these parks. Thank you!